To: Bob Boyd

From Tom + Nancy Rocicka
Aug 2002 (Vail, Co)

PERRY MAXWELL'S PRAIRIE DUNES

PERRY MAXWELL'S PRAIRIE DUNES

Mal Elliott / photography by John R. Johnson

Sleeping Bear Press

Frontispiece: View of the 11th and 16th holes from the native grass rough that typifies the character of Prairie Dunes (John R. Johnson/golfphoto).

Sleeping Bear Press
310 North Main Street
P.O. Box 20
Chelsea, MI 48118
www.sleepingbearpress.com

Printed and bound in Canada

10 9 8 7 6 5 4 3 2 1

Library of Congress Cataloging-in-Publication Data

Elliott, James M.
Perry Maxwell's Prairie Dunes / by James M. Elliott ;
Photography by John R. Johnson.
p. cm.
ISBN 1-58536-073-2
1. Prairie Dunes (Golf Course : Hutchinson, Kan.)--History.
2. Maxwell, Perry. I. Title: Prairie Dunes. II. Title.
GV969.P64 E55 2002
796.352'09781'83--dc21
2002004305

*For color photography orders contact: Johnson Design Golf Marketing
(206) 324-2442 or www.golfphotos.com*

This book would not have been completed without the help of many people, most of whom have a deep knowledge of and love for Prairie Dunes Country Club.

❧❧

Bob Gilliland, former Prairie Dunes historian and longtime member; Jane Hart, current club historian; Howard J. "Jake" Carey Jr., Prairie Dunes charter member and nephew of founders; Charles Craig, Prairie Dunes head professional; Stan George, Prairie Dunes golf course superintendent; Randy Hunt, general manager, Prairie Dunes Country Club; Dora Deskins Horn, Perry Maxwell's granddaughter; Dora Maxwell Harrison, Perry Maxwell's daughter; Hodie Maxwell, widow of J. Press Maxwell; Jerry Westheimer, son-in-law of Dean Woods, Perry Maxwell's construction engineer; Jerry Westheimer Jr., grandson of Dean Woods; Jim Misunas, golf writer for the *Hutchinson News*; Ken MacLeod, editor, *South Central Golf* magazine; Fran Elliott, researcher and proofreader.

{ FOREWORD }

By Judy Bell

Prairie Dunes and I were conceived in the same year, 1936. I arrived in the fall of 1936 and Prairie Dunes opened in 1937.

Until 2002, Prairie Dunes was one of the best-kept secrets in American golf. While it has hosted three United States Women's Amateur Championships, a U. S. Mid-Amateur Championship, a USGA Senior Amateur Championship, and a Curtis Cup match, it has never been the centerpiece of a telecast of a national championship. The selection of Prairie Dunes as the site of the 2002 Women's Open meant that Prairie Dunes would finally get its due. Golfers around the world would be able to see the finest women players in the world test their skills over this magnificent set of holes. And it was hoped that Kansas would be hospitable enough to produce a few Kansas gales, hopefully from both the north and the south, to challenge the players!

Perry Maxwell designed the original nine of Prairie Dunes, in the midst of what some refer to as the Golden Age of American golf architecture. It was, oddly, during the Great Depression that Maxwell, Donald Ross, and Alister MacKenzie created many of our finest courses. Prairie Dunes has been called a bright spot on the bleak Depression landscape.

Maxwell, in fact, was probably the most prolific golf architect in the United States during the Great Depression and ironically did most of his work in what was called the Dust Bowl – Kansas, Texas, and Oklahoma.

For 20 years the course had the reputation as the best nine-hole course in the country. Then, in 1957, Maxwell's son, J. Press Maxwell, completed the other nine. Many believe he used his father's routing plan and added some touches of his own.

I especially like the 4th, 5th 13th, 14th, and 15th holes of the new nine.

The course is a true Scottish links—an impression heightened by the severe rough. The only piece missing is the body of water alongside the links. A good links is one where a golfer can stand on a teeing ground and see several holes. This is exactly the case at Prairie Dunes.

The par-4 8th and the par-3 10th, particularly, are classic holes that Scotland would be proud of. Natural plum thickets abound, enhancing the seaside impression of the course and pot bunkers enhance the striking links-like qualities.

Perry Maxwell's reputation included being noted for his severely contoured greens, even having them dubbed "the Maxwell Rolls." These Maxwell touches are much in evidence at Prairie Dunes.

Since the course is only 40 miles from Wichita, where I grew up, I became aware of Prairie Dunes when I was around 12 years old. The first time I played the course, I knew it was the best I had ever seen, even though it was only nine holes. Dave Truffelli and Mike Murra, the two men who taught me how to play, would take me to Prairie Dunes for a game. I still remember how excited I would be to play there. Over the years, I have probably played 200 rounds on this magnificent links-like design and, I must say, in my mind a perfect day of golf is the unmatched challenge of a round at Prairie Dunes. Mal Elliott's attention to detail and excellent writing style make this book a must-read for friends of the game.

COLORADO SPRINGS, CO
SPRING 2002
USGA PRESIDENT, 1996-97

Despite having one of the world's great architects in Perry Maxwell and one of the world's ideal settings, Prairie Dunes Country Club got off to a slow start on its way to a sterling international reputation.

The quality of the course was never in question. The location in a remote spot in the middle of Kansas was one problem. Another was the fact that for the first 20 years of its existence the course included only nine holes.

This meant that Prairie Dunes lacked exposure. The reputation of the nine-hole course in Kansas grew by word of mouth, but few of the nation's top players had seen it with their own eyes.

The city of Hutchinson had been at the forefront of the game of golf in the state of Kansas and the region since the

Prairie Dunes flagstick and cup.
(John R. Johnson/golfphotos)

turn of the century. Hutchinson Country Club was one of the five founding members of the Kansas Golf Association in 1908. Hutchinson was also the site of six men's and four women's state championship tournaments prior to the completion of Prairie Dunes in 1937.

In 1938 the Kansas Golf Association staged its state championship at Prairie Dunes, despite the fact that there were only nine holes. But it would not return again until 1962. When the course attained a full complement of 18 holes in 1957, it immediately attracted its first nationally important event, the 1958 men's Trans-Mississippi.

Founders William and June Carey had plans to add nine

holes much earlier, and even mentioned building an additional 18 holes. That was two decades before the 18-hole layout was completed. Around 1940, severe weather left the course in poor condition. Then came World War II, which put a damper on nearly all golf activities.

As a result, it was 1957 before Prairie Dunes became a real presence in the world of golf. Yes, Walker Cupper Johnny Dawson gave it his endorsement as the best nine-hole course in America, but Prairie Dunes was not taken seriously until the additional nine holes were completed.

J. Press Maxwell's work finished what his father had started. And that is when Prairie Dunes burst upon the national scene, five years after the death of its creator. Not being located near a major urban center was still a bit of a hindrance, but the Trans-Mississippi Golf Association gave the course exposure to some of the best golfers in the

The modest Prairie Dunes clubhouse and two giant cottonwood trees in the evening sun. (John R. Johnson/golfphotos)

Midwest and the nation. It didn't hurt that a fellow named Nicklaus won the title.

Then June Carey and his nephew, Jake Carey, became workers and officers of the U.S. Golf Association, and Prairie Dunes jumped to a new level of respect. The course was selected as the site of several USGA events and that was the start of its climb in national and world rankings.

After a fitful start, Prairie Dunes gathered momentum, culminating in its being selected as the site of the 2002 U.S. Women's Open championship. That meant the world would see via television exposure and the written and spoken word what those who had experienced the course first-hand had known for years—that Prairie Dunes can hold its own with virtually any layout anywhere and against some of the best shotmakers in the game.

Detailed here are the events, circumstances, and the genius behind the rise of a golf course on the Kansas prairie to a position of international acclaim. This book provides a look at the two-decade delay of the completion of the course and the mystery surrounding the development of the additional nine holes in 1957.

Chapter One

⟨ THE FOUNDERS ⟩

From the turn of the twentieth century, members of the Carey family were the preeminent influence on the game of golf and many other affairs in the city of Hutchinson, Kansas. They also wielded considerable influence on the game of golf through regional and national governing bodies.

The Careys were not just avid golfers. They were golf zealots. Their infatuation with spreading the enjoyment of the game approached missionary proportions. In 1929 Hutchinson had six golf courses, the same number as Wichita and one more than Kansas City, both of which were much larger cities. This was a result of the Careys' involvement in the building of many of the layouts.

Two members of the family became influential figures in the U.S. Golf Association and Howard J. (Jake) Carey Jr. figured prominently in the Augusta National Golf Club, which stages the highly respected Masters Tournament.

Jake Carey said he does not know how his grandfather,

Emerson Carey, caught the golf bug. He only knows that the elder Carey was involved in the game long before his children began to arrive.

"He was a country club member. He was left-handed and he was a good golfer," said Jake Carey.

Emerson Carey also built an empire in the salt business, mining the massive deposits of salt which lie deep under the streets of Hutchinson, and creating the Carey Salt Company.

Emerson Carey and his four sons were involved in five different courses that were built in Hutchinson—the original Hutchinson Country Club; Willowbrook and Island Park, two private residential courses; Carey Lake Course and Golf Club; and Prairie Dunes Country Club.

When Hutchinson Country Club relocated outside the city limits in the early 1920s, Emerson Carey did not like the club's new location, so he built Willowbrook, his own private course, which adjoined his home property. It is still in operation and is enjoyed by residents of an upscale Hutchinson addition, including Howard "Jake" Carey.

Emerson Carey did not drink or smoke and he refused to gamble on his prowess as a golfer, according to acquaintances and his grandson, Jake Carey. He would occasionally allow the loser to buy him a cold drink after the round.

Another strong influence on Hutchinson golf in the early years was Harry Robb, a Scotsman who was an outstanding architect in his own right. He was the pro at Hutchinson Country Club from 1912 to 1916. He laid out courses in western Kansas and with the help of the railroads for transportation, simultaneously served as pro in three other Kansas towns.

Robb designed courses in nine Kansas towns, including Kansas City and Topeka.

In spite of the influence of Robb and the elder Carey, Hutchinson entered the 1930s without a course to which it could point with pride. This situation was soon to be remedied.

The creation of Prairie Dunes gave the city and the state of

Emerson Carey Sr., Kansas golfing and salt-mining pioneer. (Prairie Dunes)

Kansas a course destined to receive international acclaim. Its creation was no coincidence. It was the result of the collision of the kindred desires of three men who espoused respect for the roots of the game.

William D. P. Carey, the second son of Emerson, was a Rhodes scholar who studied at Oxford. In the 1920s Emerson and his youngest son, Emerson Jr., traveled to England to visit the Oxford scholar. The three played and became enamored of the Scottish golf courses.

After becoming familiar with the Scottish layouts, William became convinced that the sand dunes near his hometown had great potential to become a United States course that could approach the quality and stature of those in Scotland.

He returned to Hutchinson and joined a law firm that represented the Carey Salt Company. Emerson Jr., familiarly known as "June," also joined the law firm and he and his brother began to hatch the plan for a Scottish type of golf course.

Both William and June Carey attended Cornell University and played on the football team. June was a second-team

All-American on the 1926 team of Coach Gil "Gloomy" Dobie.

In a family of good golfers, June Carey was the outstanding player. He won the Kansas Amateur tournament in 1931 and 1935, was runner-up in 1930, was a constant threat in regional competition, and appeared in U.S. Amateur tournaments as late as the early 1950s.

June Carey also dabbled in golf course design, helping lay out the Hutchinson municipal course in 1933.

He also became a member of the USGA Executive Committee, serving six years and rising to the position of vice-president in 1960.

William Carey was a former president and a lifetime director of the Trans-Mississippi Golf Association, but most of his energies were poured into business. In addition to his legal affairs, he was involved in several business ventures, the largest of which was the Packaging Corporation of America (PCA), which he served as president. PCA merged with Tenneco, and William served as senior executive vice-president of that corporation in the 1960s.

William D. P. Carey,
Rhodes Scholar and golf
visionary. (Prairie Dunes)

He was a cofounder and president of Kansas' first television station, KTVH in Hutchinson. He also spearheaded financial drives for a local hospital and convinced the Methodist and Catholic hospitals to merge into one facility in order to provide improved service to the community. William died in 1973 at age 72.

June became an insurance executive and moved to Denver but maintained his interest in golf until his death, at age 77, in 1983.

It was no coincidence that the man who was destined to carry the Carey brothers' dreams to fruition was a golf course architect who was turning a lot of heads in nearby Oklahoma. His name was Perry Duke Maxwell. His parents came from Scotland and he had made a pilgrimmage to Scotland around 1920 to study the old courses.

Maxwell laid out courses in Tulsa and Oklahoma City that were causing a stir in golf circles. The one that caused the earliest commotion was Twin Hills Country Club in Oklahoma City, which hosted the 1935 PGA Championship.

The runner-up to June Carey in the 1931 Kansas

Amateur championship was Harry Strassburg, a clothing merchant from Coffeyville, Kansas. Strassburg was appointed by fellow members of his Hillcrest Country Club in Coffeyville to retain Maxwell to redesign their nine-hole layout in 1932.

Strassburg told a Coffeyville newspaper reporter that the Careys introduced him to Maxwell. Therefore it is clear that the Carey brothers became friends with Maxwell several years before they asked him to lay out their dream course.

By 1935 William and June Carey were ready. They called on Maxwell to look over their prospective site north of the city. Maxwell came and tramped for days through the sand dunes. He finally told the Careys that he felt the more ideal site was one several miles east of the one they had selected. He had spotted the land as he rode the train into Hutchinson.

He was ecstatic, as if he had discovered golf's Shangri-La. When asked if there were 18 good golf holes there, he uttered his now-famous reply, "There are 118 good holes

Emerson Carey Jr., football star and former USGA vice-president. (Prairie Dunes)

there. I just have to eliminate 100 of them."

It was a defining moment. Maxwell had been preaching that the lay of the land was the prerequisite to a great golf course, and here was what he considered the ideal tract over which he could route a layout that would rival those he had found on his pilgrimage to Scotland.

This occurred during the midst of the Great Depression, and even though the Carey family's diversified enterprises were not as hard hit as some, they asked Maxwell to lay out 18 holes but opted to build only nine holes.

The Careys acted at a time when Maxwell was reaching his zenith in creativity. He had spent the early 1930s in partnership with Dr. Alister MacKenzie, revered as one of the world's premier golf course architects. In 1936 Maxwell completed the design of the new Southern Hills Country Club course in Tulsa, a layout destined to become one of the world's finest and host to two U.S. Opens, the most recent one in 2001.

In 1937 he completed Prairie Dunes. Thus he created two of his most revered works just one year apart. It was also in the 1930s that he completed his most celebrated redesigns of two of the nation's most hallowed courses—Pine Valley (1933) and Augusta National (1937).

He was the most prolific of the nation's golf course architects during the hard times of the 1930s.

Prairie Dunes was one of four Kansas projects undertaken by Maxwell in the 1930s. The others were the Arkansas City Country Club, redesign of the Hillcrest Country Club course in Coffeyville, and the redesign and addition of nine holes to the Topeka Country Club course in the state's capital.

On September 13, 1937, the official opening of Prairie Dunes featured a match by a foursome comprised of Johnny Dawson, nationally prominent amateur and eventual Walker Cupper of Chicago; Ross Wilson, Prairie Dunes club pro; Ray Hockaday, Hutchinson golfer; and Dean Woods, Maxwell's brother-in-law and his construction engineer.

In Hutchinson, Maxwell's work was so brilliantly con-

Howard J. (Jake) Carey Jr.
USGA and Masters
tournament official.
(Prairie Dunes)

ceived that Prairie Dunes was the talk of the nation. Dawson called it the best nine-hole course in America.

╡ THE CLUB ╞

The Carey brothers formed the Prairie Dunes Golf Course with 110 members paying dues of $89 per year (*Prairie Dunes, the First 50 Years,* p. 95).

During the World War II years (1942-45) most golf activities were at a virtual standstill. Gasoline, rubber for golf balls, equipment, and manpower were all needed for the war effort.

The Careys nursed the club through the war years. In 1950 they offered to sell the club and the land to the members for $95,000 on a 4%, long-term note (*Prairie Dunes, the First 50 Years,* p. 96).

Jake Carey was a member of the committee formed to plan the new organization and is still a member today.

The seven incorporators who signed the papers on May 24, 1950, were J. V. Fleming, Howard J. Carey Jr., J. P. Harris, Jack C. Davis, J. P. O'Sullivan, Louis Scruggs, and Ray Dillon.

Although Prairie Dunes officially opened in 1937, it wasn't until 1950 that the club officially incorporated. The Carey family owned the course from the beginning and was responsible for most of the care and expenses to run the club. Finally, though, the club members mustered enough financial support to accept the Carey family's offer to sell the property. This is a reproduction of what the Articles of Incorporation looked like when the transfer of ownership took place.

We, the undersigned incorporators, do hereby associate ourselves together to form and establish a corporation NOT FOR PROFIT under the laws of the State of Kansas.

FIRST: The name of the corporation is PRAIRIE DUNES, INC.

SECOND: The location of its principal place of business in this state is R.F.D.4, Hutchinson, Reno County, Kansas.

THIRD: The location of its registered office in this state is R.F.D.4, Hutchinson, Reno County, Kansas.

FOURTH: The name and address of its resident agent is C.E. Chalfant, 502 First National Bank Building, Hutchinson, Kansas.

FIFTH: This corporation is organized NOT FOR PROFIT and the nature of its business is:

(a) To maintain and operate a club for social enjoyment and to maintain a club-house and golf course and other recreational and social facilities for the convenience of the members.

(b) To encourage, develop, and promote recreational and social activities for the benefit and pleasure of the members of the club.

(c) To purchase or otherwise acquire, hold, operate, manage, lease, mortgage and otherwise encumber, plat, sub-divide, develop, improve, sell, convey, exchange, use and dispose of real estate or personal property or any rights or interest therein.

(d) To, subject to the laws of Kansas now or hereafter in effect, purchase, sell and transfer memberships in the corporation, PROVIDED that the memberships belonging to the corporation shall not be voted on directly or indirectly.

(e) To exercise all powers conferred upon corporations by the laws of the State of Kansas, now or hereafter in effect, for the accomplishment of the purposes and the carrying on and promotion of the business and objects of this corporation.

SIXTH: This corporation shall not have authority to issue capital stock.

SEVENTH: The conditions of membership shall be fixed by the By-Laws of the corporation.

EIGHTH: The names and places of residence (post office address) of each of the incorporators are as follows:

J.V. Fleming, Wiley Building, Hutchinson, Kansas, Howard J. Carey, Jr., Avenue B & Poplar, Hutchinson, Kansas, J.P. Harris, 28 East Second, Hutchinson, Kansas, Jack C. Davis, 732 East First, Hutchinson, Kansas, J.P. O'Sullivan, Avenue D & Washington, Hutchinson, KS, Louis Scruggs, 729 South Main, Hutchinson, Kansas, Ray Dillon, Jr., 307 North Washington, Hutchinson, Kansas.

NINTH: The term for which this corporation is to exist is One Hundred Years.

> ❧ ARTICLES OF INCORPORATION *continued* ❧
>
> TENTH: The number of Trustees shall be Seven.
>
> IN TESTIMONY WHEREOF: We have hereunto subscribed our names, this 24th day of May, 1950.
>
> J.V. Fleming
Howard J. Carey, Jr.

Jake Carey carried on the family tradition in golf. In 1950 he was elected a director of the Trans-Mississippi Golf Association. He eventually served seven years on the USGA Executive Committee, acting as chairman of the Senior Championship Committee and the Public Links Committee. He helped bring several Trans-Mississippi and USGA events to Prairie Dunes.

He also became a fixture at the Masters Tournament. He is one of only three Kansans admitted to the exclusive Augusta National Golf Club that sponsors the Masters. For 23 years he served on the rules committee at the Masters, from 1975 to 1998.

By 1955 the Prairie Dunes members decided that their esteemed nine-hole layout should be expanded to 18 holes. They raised $122,500 to build the additional holes and enlarge the clubhouse.

Maxwell had died in 1952. The man they chose to redesign the course was his son, Press Maxwell, who rejoined his father's business after returning from a colorful and heroic stint as a bomber pilot in World War II. The cost of the additional holes was $47,500 (*Prairie Dunes, the First 50 Years,* p. 97).

The new layout opened June 2, 1957, with a field of 60 in a

pro-amateur event. Ted Gwin, head pro at a Wichita club, fashioned an impressive 3-under-par 67 to win low pro honors. It would prove to be one of the best rounds on the course during the ensuing years.

The national and international fame of Prairie Dunes makes it a club of wide influence. Eminent figures in the world of golf and business purchase memberships in the club for the chance to play the course when their travels take them near Hutchinson. Almost any day you can find men and women from various locations around the country testing the hallowed course.

Since the club created a nonresident category of membership, the limit of 100 has not only been fully subscribed but there is also a waiting list. In order to be a nonresident member, one cannot live closer than 125 miles to Hutchinson.

Over the years, Prairie Dunes has contributed significantly to the game of golf. Judy Bell of Wichita, who in 1996–1997 became the first, and only woman to date, president of the USGA, is a member of Prairie Dunes. June, William, and Jake Carey were prominent officials in the USGA, Trans-Mississippi, and Masters Tournament.

Prairie Dunes Country Club and all that the mention of the name evokes resulted from the dedication and hard work of the Carey family and their love of the game of golf. A plaque on the stone wall at the entrance to the course captures that thought.

Plaque at the club entrance honoring the Carey family. (Prairie Dunes)

Chapter Two

{ THE MAXWELLS: FATHER AND SON ARCHITECTS }

Perry Maxwell told Bill Inglish of the Daily Oklahoman *in 1950 that
Prairie Dunes "is the nicest canvas on which I've ever painted a picture."*

Many golfers and admirers have portrayed Perry Maxwell as an "artist." His comment to Inglish, the former official statistician of the Masters Tournament, is proof that the famous golf architect viewed himself in the same light.

Maxwell and his family were lovers of art in all its forms—painting, music, and golf course architecture. His wife Ray was an artist, as was daughter Mary Belle, who studied at the Sorbonne in Paris. His daughter Dora studied photography under George Platt Lynes, one of the nation's more famous photographers in New York City.

So when Maxwell first sketched out a new hole, he was painting a picture. A streak of fairway here, a splash of green there, surrounded by a touch of tan in a bunker. Nothing obtrusive or garish. He didn't work in oils, but in soils and grasses. Maxwell was also a lover of the handiwork of God and nature.

When you drive onto the Prairie Dunes grounds, you have to strain to detect the presence of any golf course. The seventh green and a practice green are visible near the clubhouse. The rest of the course is out there lying in wait, virtually unseen from the road. Even the ninth green, the one that sits only about 40 yards from the front of the clubhouse, rests behind a screen of tall grass and other prairie flora.

Perry Duke Maxwell was known to his close friends and associates as "P. D." How appropriate that those are also the initials of Prairie Dunes, the course that brought him and the town of Hutchinson so much acclaim.

Maxwell has received many accolades for his single-minded

pursuit of excellence in course design. He was one of the earliest American-born architects to rise to the level of admiration and respect accorded to Scotsmen Alister MacKenzie and Donald Ross.

Maxwell became one of the two most respected American-born golf course designers in the pre-World War II era. The other was A. W. Tillinghast of Philadelphia, a flamboyant and tragic figure. There were other outstanding designers, but Maxwell and Tillinghast left the largest number of layouts that have withstood the test of time and the judgment of the sport's collective minds.

One of Maxwell's highest compliments came from MacKenzie himself in a remark made to Dr. Charles Evans, former superintendent of schools in Maxwell's home town of Marion, Kentucky, and later secretary of the Oklahoma Historical Society.

Maxwell introduced MacKenzie to Evans at the Skirvin Tower Hotel in Oklahoma City and in so doing praised MacKenzie for his world reputation in golf. Evans wrote: "The Scot, with true brogue, turned to me and said, 'Mr. Maxwell speaks of my ability to make a good fairway or develop a worthy green, but I wish to tell you that in laying

Perry Duke Maxwell. (Dora Maxwell Harrison)

out a golf course and to give it everything that the science and art of golf demand, Mr. Maxwell is not second to anyone I know.' " *(Chronicles of Oklahoma,* Spring, 1953, Vol. XXXI, Number 1).

Maxwell's accomplishments came despite a lifetime of health problems. He had tuberculosis as a young man, which interfered with his college education. He also lost a leg in 1944 as a result of complications from an X-ray burn in his younger days.

In many ways, Maxwell was an enigma. He regained his health sufficiently to become an accomplished player in tennis, a sport that requires stamina and aerobic fitness. Friends and relatives said he never drank or smoked, but his daughter said he had a bad habit of constantly chewing on a pencil.

His first wife, Ray Woods, was a genteel woman. It was she who showed him an article on the new National Golf Links on Long Island, New York, that was completed in 1911. He traveled cross-country by train to investigate the course and returned to Ardmore to begin building Dornick Hills.

Maxwell said his wife thought that golf would be easier on him than tennis, which he had played most of his life. The Maxwell home in Ardmore sported a clay court, according to his daughter Dora, who was also a tennis player.

Maxwell was the son of a physician and attended college at Kentucky University and Stetson University in Florida. His poor health kept him from completing his formal education but he was widely known as a voracious reader and a well-educated man.

His father, Dr. James Maxwell, died when Perry was nine and his mother and his uncle, Presley Maxwell, raised him. The uncle, a man of some means, never married. He obtained property in Harris County, Texas, near Houston. When he died, the inheritance left Perry's family well financed.

The Perry Maxwell birthplace in Princeton, Ky.
(Courtesy Dora Horn)

Perry visited Ardmore, Indian Territory, and decided the climate would be good for his health. In 1904, he moved to Indian Territory and his uncle bought for him several shares in the Ardmore National Bank where he eventually became a vice-president.

Banking apparently was not his niche, however, and his wife, Ray, was well aware of it. She pointed out to him the article on the National Golf Links of America in New York, and he scheduled a trip to look at it. It would turn out to be a trip that would change the lifeworks of Perry Maxwell. He was so enamored of golf course design following that excursion east that it prompted him to move into the design business.

Maxwell said in a later interview that there was only one book on golf course architecture when he started out, and he read it.

In 1914, Maxwell traveled to Manchester, Vermont, to attend the U.S. Amateur tournament and to watch Francis Ouimet, who had stunned the golf world by beating the pros to win the 1913 U.S. Open. With the help of Ouimet, whom he had come to know, Maxwell picked out a set of clubs, which he purchased for $9, and began to play (*Golf*

Perry Maxwell and daughter Elizabeth in Ardmore, Okla., circa 1909. (Courtesy Dora Horn)

Digest, August, 1982).

Back home, he designed and began construction of Dornick Hills Country Club in Ardmore. The family, including the three girls, picked up the small rocks that covered the foothills of the Arbuckle Mountains. The work began in 1913 and the first nine holes were completed in 1918. When his wife died in 1919, Maxwell was heartbroken.

Dr. Evans gave the eulogy at the funeral. In a tribute written for the Ardmore newspaper, he recalled Maxwell's words that day, "I am going to place her form out yonder on the golf course which we shaped in love together; high up on the long ridge bordered by bold oaks she will rest and I shall build an archway there, perhaps a nameless one, but it will tell of my silent and everlasting devotion."

Above left: Perry Duke Maxwell at age 25 as a young banker in Indian Territory. (Courtesy Dora Horn) Above right: Mrs. Ray Woods Maxwell. (Courtesy Dora Horn)

He built the shrine near the tee of the seventh hole at Dornick Hills. It consists of a semicircle of columns reminiscent of Greek architecture. That spot has since become a family burial plot and a picnic area. Maxwell and his wife are buried there, along with daughters Mary Belle and Elizabeth, his wife's mother and father, and one of her brothers.

In order to take his mind off his loss, he traveled to Scotland, where he studied the golf architecture and where he first met Alister MacKenzie (*Golf Digest,* August, 1982).

At the age of 40, Maxwell cut back his activities at the bank and poured his entire passion into course design. He did not abandon banking entirely until 1929 at age 50.

Although Dornick Hills was his first effort at design, it became his trademark effort. He grasped quickly the principles

The Maxwell burial place and memorial to Mrs. Ray Woods Maxwell.

(*Courtesy the* Daily Ardmoreite)

by which he would design his most honored layouts. This was evident from the remarks he made in an interview for a photo-biography in *The American Golfer* magazine in the spring of 1935.

"The minimum of expense was the first consideration," he said. "That, and the importance of creating a course that would be a legitimate tax upon the skill of the players."

This was his mind-set as he designed Dornick Hills.

"It was my wife's suggestion that Ardmore be built," Maxwell said. "She did not live to see the course completed. I have since made golf architecture my lifework, having built several along the lines of Ardmore, never, at any time attempting a piece of property devoid of natural features."

This lays out his firm belief that the land makes the course. It is no coincidence that the names of his early courses nearly always included the word "hills." After Dornick Hills came Twin Hills Country Club in Oklahoma City, and Indian Hills and Southern Hills in Tulsa. The dunes in Prairie Dunes continued the same theme.

"It is my theory that nature must precede the architect, in the laying out of links," said Maxwell. "It is futile to attempt the transformation of wholly inadequate acres into an adequate course."

His philosophy was diametrically opposed to that of Charles "Steam Shovel" Banks, who believed in moving massive amounts of earth in building gigantic, elevated greens and yawning bunkers in the 1920s.

"A featureless site cannot possibly be economically redeemed," Maxwell was quoted as saying in *The American Golfer* article. "Many an acre of magnificent land has been utterly destroyed by the steam shovel, throwing up its billows of earth, biting out traps and bunkers, transposing landmarks that are contemporaries of Genesis."

Maxwell likened the effort of attempting to remold featureless land into an interesting layout as "the inauguration of an earthquake. The site of a golf course should *be* there, not be *brought* there."

Maxwell was passionately adamant about his stand on minimal interference with nature. He said the engineers, surveyors, and landscape experts cannot be blamed for carrying out the designs on the blueprints, most of which he said, "come into existence at the instigation of amateurs obsessed with a passion for remodeling the masterpieces of nature. A golf course that invades a hundred or more acres, and is actually visible in its garish intrusion from several points of observation is an abhorrent spectacle. The less of man's handiwork, the better a course."

Prairie Dunes, more than any of his other works, carries out that philosophy to the fullest. There was no heavy equipment used. The work was done with mules and Fresno scrapers and Works Progress Administration (WPA) labor. The holes, particularly the original nine, blend into the landscape so subtly that from a distance you must look closely to detect them.

The timing of Maxwell's entry into the field of golf course architecture was good, because in the 1920s America had a love affair with the game of golf so intense that it is difficult today to comprehend. Many colorful and larger-than-life characters dotted the golfing landscape.

The decade began with Walter Hagen as the well-established superstar, and before long amateur Bobby Jones began his string of conquests. Hagen did more than any other figure to add glamour and lofty status to the image of the professional golfer. Jones became the greatest champion of the amateur golfer since Ouimet outplayed the great British pros Harry Vardon and Ted Ray in winning the 1913 U. S. Open.

In the 1920s, there were more golf courses built in the United States than in any decade before or since. Until 1897 there were no golf courses in Kansas. Three decades later there were more than 180 (*Kansas Facts, a Yearbook of Kansas, 1929*). In Kansas, virtually every town of 1,000 or more had its own course by 1929, even though many of them were nine-hole, sand-green affairs.

Oklahoma lagged well behind Kansas in the number of golf courses but Maxwell was about to help narrow the gap. He captured more than his fair share of the jobs in his home state, and those early jobs established his superiority in fashioning Oklahoma's landscape into layouts that would be admired for ages.

Maxwell told an Oklahoma City sportswriter in 1950 that he designed 70 courses and redesigned 40 for a total of 110. He did not leave a complete list. Records indicate that he produced 51 original designs and made revisions to 26 additional courses.

In 1921, he began his first design-for-hire. He built Twin Hills Golf and Country Club in Oklahoma City, a project so widely admired that it propelled him into the limelight. Another of his early-day courses was Indian Hills in Tulsa. In 1923 he added nine holes to Dornick Hills. After that, he was in great demand.

He took on many jobs and worked relentlessly to secure projects. In the beginning he was selling himself. Floyd Farley, another prolific Oklahoma golf architect, said Maxwell worked hard at being on the spot wherever he heard someone was considering building a course.

Farley, who was the pro at Twin Hills and later built and owned an Oklahoma City course, said Maxwell would come to his shop to talk architecture. "He was an arm-waver," said Farley. "He talked with his hands."

Farley said Maxwell drew his plans at a scale of 1 inch to 100 yards as opposed to the more customary 1 inch to 200 yards. "That makes for a long piece of paper blowing in the wind when you're out on the course," said Farley.

Maxwell achieved national acclaim when he teamed with Alister MacKenzie in the early 1930s. Maxwell was a teetotaler while MacKenzie could seldom be found without a bottle of Scotch whiskey nearby. So in the matter of personal habits they were the "odd couple."

Maxwell loved to eat tomatoes with sugar and vinegar. His daughter, Dora Harrison, said MacKenzie would rib him, saying, "Perry, don't you know that vinegar puts alcohol into your stomach?"

There was nothing odd about their collaboration on design, however. They worked together on the Crystal Downs Country Club course in Frankfort, Michigan, the University of Michigan and Ohio State University courses. Crystal Downs existed in relative anonymity until it hosted the U.S. Senior Amateur Championship in 1988. With many similarities to Prairie Dunes, Crystal Downs has recently received the recognition many felt it deserved long ago. It is now ranked among the top 10 courses in the world by most major golf publications.

Ben Crenshaw, two-time Masters champion and captain of the 1999 Ryder Cup team, is a noted golf architect, historian, and student of Maxwell. He said Maxwell should get most of the credit for the work on the courses where he worked with MacKenzie. After all, it has been documented that MacKenzie typically swept into town, walked a site, quickly made his design sketches, and then left town only for the construction engineer to finish the project.

The reason for this is that Maxwell was MacKenzie's construction engineer and the man who put the finishing touches on the courses following MacKenzie's specifications. If a person has been to both Crystal Downs and Prairie Dunes, one could blindfold the individual and put him on a green, remove the blindfold to show him only the green, and it would be difficult to differentiate between the two locales.

Crenshaw's opinion carries more than just the weight of a great golfer. He is also a golf historian and has become a top course designer. He and his partner, Bill Coore, designed Sand Hills Golf Club in Mullen, Nebraska, which almost immediately broke into the top 10 in *Golf Magazine*'s top 100 United States courses, at No. 8.

In 1945 Maxwell told B. A. Bridgewater, sports editor of the *Tulsa World*, that Fielding H. "Hurry Up" Yost, the University of Michigan's director of athletics, bragged that the University course was the best in the United States.

"Which isn't true," Maxwell told Bridgewater, "although we did spend a lot of money on it. Money was no object at Michigan. They wanted something distinctive and different. So we spent $35,000 decorating the fairways with pine trees 25 and 35 feet tall. It's very pretty now."

Maxwell also built the Iowa State University course in 1934 and the personal golf course of Eugene Grace, the head of Bethlehem Steel in Pennsylvania.

It was also during the 1930s when Maxwell did two of his most famous redesigns at Pine Valley in 1933 and at Augusta National in 1937. In 1940, he lent his magic touch to a now famous stretch of holes at Colonial Country Club in Fort Worth.

Maxwell's most productive years were during the late 1920s and 1930s. He would undoubtedly have created more courses but for the Great Depression and World War II. However, dogged determination landed him more jobs during the Great Depression than most of his contemporaries.

Again, this was probably a result not only of his skill in fashioning outstanding courses but also his belief in economy, which he first practiced at Dornick Hills.

"Professionals and topnotch amateurs who have played it [Dornick Hills] pronounce the greens and fairways perfect," Maxwell told *The American Golfer*. "The total cost of construction and upkeep over a period of 11 years is less than $35,000. By that I mean about $3,000 per annum. Nature has been kind, because we have not defied her. We cooperate with the seasons, and dividends never fail."

Maxwell was not an outstanding golfer. It was said he was a better tennis player than a golfer. Charlie Coe, two-time U.S. Amateur champion, grew up in Ardmore playing Dornick Hills and was a friend of Maxwell.

Coe said Maxwell was a family golfer who played the game with his wife and kids. But Coe deeply respected Maxwell's ability to lay out a golf course (*Daily Oklahoman*, May 23, 1993).

Maxwell's effect on golf course architecture was profound. So was his thinking on many subjects. Press Maxwell's wife, Kathryn, familiarly known as "Hodie," provided a glimpse into the complex nature of her father-in-law. She said he once gave her as a birthday present a book by the German philosopher Immanuel Kant. "Kant was one of his favorites," she said.

Dr. Evans wrote, "Dean Julian Monnet of the University of Oklahoma once said to me, 'I have just had a long visit with Perry Maxwell. Do you know that the more I am associated with him, the more thoroughly I am convinced that he is one of the most learned men I have met.' "

Maxwell's second wife, Josie, was a pianist who had trained at the Juilliard School of Music. She and her first husband, Bill Hume, were close friends of the Maxwells before they moved from Ardmore to Tulsa. She and Maxwell were married after her husband died.

Few people knew the extent to which Maxwell suffered with his bad leg. The mishap with X-ray burns in the 1920s left him with severe eczema on the leg. His daughter, Dora Harrison, said her father was constantly caring for the leg. He loved wool suits but could not allow the wool to touch his skin so he wore cotton pajama bottoms under his trousers.

Problems with his leg took him frequently to Philadelphia where he received treatments from a well-known dermatologist. While there, he would attend the opera and the symphony and buy imported wool suits.

"One time he went to Philadelphia and tried to attend the opera, but it was sold out," said Dora Harrison. "He told them, 'But I came all the way from Oklahoma.' They found him a seat."

His physical handicap did not halt his pursuit of his beloved occupation. He designed or redesigned some 20 golf courses between the end of World War II and his death in 1952.

Since the Maxwell children were motherless, an aunt cared for them while their father was busy designing golf courses. Then they attended boarding schools.

Maxwell's two elder daughters, Elizabeth and Mary Belle, graduated from Wellesley, an exclusive women's college. His daughter Dora also studied at Wellesley and son Press attended Dartmouth, an Ivy League school in Hanover,

New Hampshire.

Mary Belle helped her father with sketches of Maxwell golf holes, particularly ones he was redesigning.

Dora Harrison points out that it was difficult for her father to send four children to college, especially during the Depression. Fortunately, Maxwell lived and worked in a rare pocket of moderate prosperity during the hard times. If he hadn't, he might have had no work at all. The oil business was almost Depression-proof and in Oklahoma it provided much of his employment. And the Carey family's success with Hutchinson's salt mines helped provide funds for Prairie Dunes.

Another positive factor of the time was the Works Progress Administration of the Franklin D. Roosevelt administration. The WPA provided most of the labor for both Southern Hills and Prairie Dunes.

Perry Maxwell (left), Mary Belle sketching a hole for redesign, and Press. (Courtesy Dora Harrison)

But Southern Hills and Prairie Dunes provided Maxwell more than money. They provided the settings where he could conceive an artistic breakthrough that would preserve his image for posterity.

Those Depression-era projects did not exactly line Maxwell's pockets. There is no exact record of what he was paid for Prairie Dunes but it is almost certain that it would have been a modest sum.

Also, there is little doubt that Maxwell's penchant for pinching pennies had a significant impact on his ability to land jobs in the hard times of the 1930s.

Maxwell designed Southern Hills for a fee of just $7,500 and built the entire project for just more than $100,000. Records have not been found but logic would say he received even less for Prairie Dunes, since he routed 18 holes but completed only nine holes. When the Carey

Perry Maxwell relaxing on the beach in Clearwater, Fla., in 1940,
where he was redesigning four holes. (Courtesy Dora Horn)

brothers sold the club to the members in 1950, it was specu-
lated that the $95,000 selling price was what the project
had cost, including the cost of the clubhouse.

This is not out of line with what MacKenzie wrote in his
book, *The Spirit of St. Andrews,* in the early 1930s. He wrote,
"If a club had only $30,000 to build a course, the greens and
bunkers, hillocks and hollows could be done for $10,000,
the drainage and irrigation for $10,000 and the seeding for
$2,000, leaving $8,000 for the architect's fees, fertilizers
and other necessities."

Using that as a gauge, $7,000 seems a likely figure for an
architect's fee of that era.

Maxwell would occasionally accept a tract of land as part
of his payment. According to his granddaughter, Dora
Horn, a part of his estate when he died in 1952 was property
in Frankfort, Michigan, near the project where he assisted
MacKenzie at Crystal Downs.

One avenue utilized by Maxwell that saved his clients
money was with an economy of bunkers. Large numbers of
bunkers were not only unnecessary but also undesirable, in
his view. He made this clear in the article in *The American
Golfer.* It was written in the spring of 1935. This was before

he completed Southern Hills and Prairie Dunes and before he pulled off his much-heralded revision of the greens at Augusta National in 1937. Yet he had already attracted a large following.

"Far too many (bunkers) exist in our land," he said, pointing out that the Oakmont Country Club, which was to host the 1935 U. S. Open, had 200 bunkers.

"Other courses famed everywhere average 150," he said. "From 20 to 25, plus the natural obstacles, are ample for any course. Millions of dollars annually are wasted in devastating the earth; in obstructing the flow of the rainfall; in creating impossible conditions.

"Don't blame all of this on the architects; the guilt lies primarily with the influential, misguided club members who take sadistic joy in torturing the good earth. As a result, the majority of American golf clubs are in the red."

He likened the red to "the gore of the steam shovel, blood drawn by the mound builders." Maxwell had a frequent reminder of this imagery in his native Oklahoma where much of the soil is bright red clay.

As his daughter-in-law Hodie Maxwell said, "He always stood for something, unlike so many today." And from his comments it is clear one always knew where he stood.

After the addition of nine holes in 1957, Prairie Dunes had only 64 bunkers. A few more have been added, not to alter strategy, but for utilitarian reasons. Yet the total is still just 79. How many of these are not natural bunkers is not clear after the passage of more than 60 years.

Maxwell further indicted the American game of the 1930s by saying, "We have learned nothing from Scotland or England, where the ancient and honorable game can be enjoyed on marvelous links at one-tenth the admission fees, dues, green fees, etc., that prevail in the land of the free."

That was in 1935. What would Maxwell think of the cost to play the game today?

There is a lot of emphasis today on the desirability of trees and water on a golf course. When Maxwell designed Prairie Dunes there were virtually no trees. Even today, trees do not come into play prominently except on No. 12, where a large cottonwood in the right center of the fairway guards the entrance to the green, some 90 yards away. Also, there is only one body of water on the course and it does not come into play.

A big concern of the Carey brothers was that there be no parallel fairways, no out-of-bounds and no water holes, according to Steve Horrell, a former football teammate of William Carey at Cornell. Horrell became an executive in the Carey Salt Company. He said the Careys also wanted no houses and no trees except those that were there naturally (*Prairie Dunes, the First 50 Years*, p. 15).

Although Maxwell did not address the subject of trees, MacKenzie, his world-renowned partner of the early 1930s, did. He wrote that some golfers in his day actually condemned trees. However, MacKenzie insisted that on inland courses, the use of trees was the only way to provide hazards as high as the sand dunes.

This was written in 1932. MacKenzie did not live to see the creation of Prairie Dunes, and thus missed witnessing a titillating exception to that observation.

Even though he endorsed some use of trees, MacKenzie preferred small groups strategically located. Playing down fairways bordered by straight lines of trees he viewed as being not only "inartistic but also tedious and uninteresting."

Maxwell and MacKenzie worked so closely together for several years it is safe to assume that their opinions on trees were similar.

Some clientele like the Careys and the Southern Hills group had the insight to appreciate Maxwell's acumen, but on the whole, golf course architects were vastly overlooked and undervalued in the early days except in areas and at clubs steeped in golf tradition.

With courses proliferating at such a stunning rate in the 1920s and 1930s there were not enough accomplished designers to keep pace. In many cases knowledgeable designers were brought in to do the routing but the construction was left to amateurs.

Prairie Dunes is considered Maxwell's greatest masterpiece. His daughter, Dora Harrison, said it was her father's favorite, "because it was over rough ground like the Scottish courses."

She said she knew of only one other piece of ground that her father cherished as much as Prairie Dunes. That was a stretch of beach on Barnegat Bay in New Jersey. She said the family would picnic occasionally on Barnegat Bay, and that her father had a choice spot but could never sell his idea of building a golf course there. Nor has anyone built a course in the area since.

Maxwell completed several humble layouts, some of which have been lost to memory and the record books. One was a nine-hole course in Bristow, Oklahoma, just one of many small towns in Oklahoma and Kansas which boast of a Maxwell-designed course. His work in Bristow was of his usual high quality so that the town still brags of the virtues of the course. With his demand for a quality piece of land to work, simply to be selected as a site for a Maxwell course was a compliment in itself.

But the sand dunes of Hutchinson gave him a rare opportunity with a ready-made terrain where he could practice minimal disruption of nature.

Maxwell's first effort at course design in his hometown of Ardmore provided him with an almost ideal tract that helped him become proficient at utilizing the hills. Dornick Hills Country Club sits in the foothills of Oklahoma's Arbuckle Mountains. But the sand hills of Hutchinson provided him his finest piece of raw nature on which to sculpt.

Maxwell was involved at nearly every level of the game of golf. In 1924 he served on the greens committee of the U.S. Golf Association and was president of the Oklahoma State Golf Association. He was also vice-president of the state association in 1917, 1920, and 1923.

Dickson Saunders, Perry Maxwell's Tulsa attorney, was quoted in a newspaper account (*The Daily Oklahoman,* May 23, 1993) as saying that Maxwell didn't keep records well and ran his business from his checkbook stubs.

Dora Harrison said her father's suitcase was his filing cabinet and she could not remember a year when he didn't have to ask for an extension of time to file his income tax return. He was excellent with figures but he just never got around to doing his taxes, she said.

Maxwell's great-nephew Jerry Westheimer Jr., the grandson of Dean Woods, has a commemorative medal given to Woods and Maxwell when they redesigned Colonial Country Club in Fort Worth. He said Maxwell underbid that project and it cost him $5,000 out-of-pocket. Officials of the club knew that they got a bargain, but their only response was the medal.

His old high school superintendent, Dr. Evans, said Maxwell had a head for figures. But based on Maxwell's short-lived banking career and his personal account keeping, his head and his heart were obviously in things artistic.

Maxwell was obsessed with his vocation.

Dora Harrison said the family would be driving in Oklahoma and her father would spot a golf course, stop the car, and they all had to walk on the course.

"He would kneel down and run his hands across the grass

and say, 'Girls, just *feel* these greens.'"

For the last eight years of his life, Maxwell was a familiar figure getting around golf courses on crutches. His leg was amputated in 1944 just above the knee because the damage from the X-ray burn he suffered as a young man became malignant.

Undaunted, he continued to work, although he depended more and more on his son Press.

"We kids thought the neatest thing about Grandfather was that at night he could take his leg off and stand it in the corner," recalled Dora Deskins Horn of Mesa, Arizona.

Maxwell died November 16, 1952, at his home in Tulsa. The newspaper account said he suffered a fractured vertebra in his back several months before. But the cause of death was listed as pneumonia.

He was a 33rd Degree Mason and a member of the Presbyterian Church of Ardmore. Josie Maxwell donated a stained-glass window to the church as a memorial to her

Perry Maxwell's granddaughter Dora Horn and daughter Dora Harrison. (Courtesy Dora Horn)

husband.

Although Maxwell was well versed in the classics and could quote from the great writers, he did not leave a volume of written records as did MacKenzie. He did not write for golfing publications as did Tillinghast. Maxwell was modest, reserved, and shy, according to friends and relatives.

He was a small man, but a giant in his profession who left his artistry etched gracefully across the landscape of America in the form of traditional golf courses widely admired by those who know the game best.

We never hear of Maxwell failures. Was he, like Mozart, simply an instrument through which the artistic flowed? His first effort at Dornick Hills was a full-blown success. He did not need training. He did not need a warm-up period as does a musician. He simply began producing masterpieces. Even old, revered courses designed by other outstanding architects of his day grew in magnitude after receiving Maxwell's healing touch on minor flaws.

Composers and dramatists and golf course architects who repeatedly turn out hits get plenty of attention. Maxwell's was an easy greatness.

{ PRESS MAXWELL }

"Have you ever seen the greatest course Dad built?" Press Maxwell asked Vernon B. Snell, sports editor of the Oklahoma City Times *in 1955. "I'm speaking of Prairie Dunes up in Hutchinson, Kansas."*

Press Maxwell asked the question while he was in the midst of creating the additional nine holes at Prairie Dunes. It leaves little doubt where Prairie Dunes ranked in the Maxwell family's list of priorities.

James Press Maxwell was just a baby when the Maxwell family, including Perry Maxwell's wife Ray and three daughters, were picking up rocks on the hills north of Ardmore, Oklahoma, in preparation for creating Dornick Hills

Press Maxwell age 10, in an informal photo early in his childhood. (Courtesy Dora Maxwell Harrison)

Country Club's course. But as soon as he was old enough Press joined his father in the golf course architecture business. That was in 1936 and he was just 20 years of age.

He was on the construction crew when the elder Maxwell built Southern Hills Country Club's course in Tulsa, and again in the creation of Prairie Dunes.

During World War II Press was a much decorated hero, flying B-24 Liberator bombers with the 15th Air Force stationed in Italy. He went on bombing missions and airdropped supplies behind enemy lines. In April 1944 he became part of a special unit rescuing downed pilots from behind enemy lines in the Balkan Mountains.

Press was a captain in the 376th Bomber Group and a recipient of the Purple Heart, suffering an injury during the bombing of a hotel in Italy. His widow Hodie said he always found it amusing that after all the dangerous missions he flew, he received the Purple Heart for being in a hotel restaurant eating dinner when a bomb fell.

The Air Force would not allow a man to fly more than 50 missions. According to his wife, when Press reached his limit of 50 he was not ready to come home. Instead he volunteered to be part of a special unit formed in April of 1944, under Col. George Kraigher, to fly rescue missions. Kraigher was a native Serbian who before the war was manager of Pan American Airways' western operations in Mexico, Central America, and the northern coast of South America. In 1941 he became operations manager for a Pan American subsidiary which supplied material to Great Britain, Russia, China, and sometimes across North Africa. This operation was militarized in 1944 for the rescue mission.

Kraigher was also the uncle of former Yugoslavian president Sergei Krajger.

The Yugoslavians were waging guerrilla warfare against the Nazis in Central Europe. Kraigher and Press were assigned to Marshal Tito's headquarters. They were known as Tito's "two-man air force." With the help of the Yugoslav resist-

Press Maxwell, a WWII Air Force hero. (Courtesy Dora Maxwell Harrison)

ance, they helped rescue about 250 Allied airmen downed in enemy-occupied territory and flew them to Bari, Italy (*The Litchfield Enquirer*, Litchfield, Conn., Sept. 19, 1984).

Before he returned to the United States, Press had flown 81 missions. Press's widow, Hodie, said she still has a set of wings given to her husband by Marshal Tito for his rescue efforts. He was also awarded the Distinguished Flying Cross and the Air Medal with four oak-leaf clusters.

As soon as Press returned to the United States in 1945 he married Hodie, whom he had met while stationed at Colorado Springs, Colorado, and he rejoined his father's golf course architecture business.

"That's all he ever did and all he ever wanted to do," said Hodie, who still lives on the 38-acre spread where she and Press raised Arabian horses after he retired in Morrison, Colorado, in 1974. She still has a pair of aged Arabians she plans to care for until they die.

Press worked for Perry until his father's death in 1952. He

Press Maxwell (second from left, front row) and some of his B-24 comrades. (Courtesy Hodie Maxwell)

took over the company and built 42 more golf courses and redesigned several others.

Press never lost his love of flying. He incorporated it into his business, flying to various jobs in Colorado, Oklahoma, and states on the Gulf Coast. He flew into Hutchinson on occasion.

"Press bought his first airplane off a used car lot in San Antonio," said Hodie. "It was a small Piper. He flew us to Dallas one time, to Love Field. (This was when Love Field was the primary airport in Dallas.)

"The battery conked out," she said. "Traffic was backed up and the tower kept insisting that we move the plane."

He later traded up to a Piper Malibu, then to a twin-engine Aztec, then to a Piper Sierra.

Press became a prominent architect in his own right and served as president of the American Society of Golf Course Architects in 1960.

Like his famous father, Press's best work was done at Prairie Dunes, where he weaved three outstanding holes

Press Maxwell and one of the Piper airplanes he used in his business.
(Courtesy Hodie Maxwell)

into the front nine and six more demanding holes into the back nine, which included the original Nos. 8 and 9 as the finishing holes.

Holes 3, 4, 5, and 11 have plenty of character. Hole 3 is a short par 4, usually played downwind, that entices big hitters to try to drive the green but penalizes them heavily if they miss. Hole No. 4 is built on a shelf into the side of a dune, much like the world-famous No. 2 hole, but it requires a different golf shot. And No. 5 is a long par 4 into a prevailing wind from an elevated tee to an elevated green. Hole No. 11 is the longest par 4 on the course. It demands an exact approach shot to a shallow green behind a mound that stands guard at the front of the green between two bunkers.

Although four of the original holes designed by his father get most of the praise at Prairie Dunes, the nine holes that Press conceived enhanced the masterpiece his father created in 1937.

The original nine holes are widely recognized as being the

ones that give Prairie Dunes its character. That figures. Perry Maxwell had first choice on the prime portion of the tract that was the best for a golf course.

Press Maxwell was never made a partner in his father's company. He worked for his father from 1936 until he took over the company at Perry's death in 1952, except for the time he served in World War II. During the time he was redesigning Prairie Dunes he was headquartered in Dallas and was also designing courses in Dallas, Houston, Shreveport, Louisiana, and Denver. Later he and his wife moved to Colorado Springs and he became the most prolific designer of the times in Colorado, where he created 18 courses and redesigned five others.

In addition to the 42 courses he designed and the 12 he redesigned, he collaborated with his father on 15 layouts. Two of his best-known jobs other than Prairie Dunes were designing Pecan Valley Country Club in San Antonio and reworking Cherry Hills Country Club in Denver.

Press Maxwell, like his father, was a modest and self-effacing individual. Although he established himself as one of the nation's finest golf architects, he never had illusions of greatness.

In a letter to a cousin who requested a list of the courses he designed, Press wrote, "Thank you for the interest, and for the compliment. You will be disappointed in quite a few of my designs, however, as they were dictated by time and the almighty dollar, and of course by the lack of genius that Father had."

In the creation of the additional nine, there is no indication the Prairie Dunes folk bothered him with time and cost. But Press faced some constraints. He had to make the new layout blend in with what his father had already done, and he was hampered by such mundane problems as poor drainage in one area. And except for holes 3, 4, and 5, the land that was close enough to tie in with the original nine had fewer dunes and less undulation.

Yet the result of his work at Prairie Dunes has stood the test of time and world opinion ever since he completed the addition in 1957. It was the work of the father that got the attention of the golf world and gave Prairie Dunes its beginning. But it was the work of the son that provided Prairie Dunes the added substance to compete with the great courses of the world. Together, they created one of the world's greatest golf masterpieces.

Chapter Three

❧ PLANNING AND CONSTRUCTION ❧

It seems incongruous to have one of the world's great golf courses located among sand dunes on the Kansas prairie. Now, consider this: when Prairie Dunes was conceived, it was even more remote from the city that now claims it.

In 1935 Prairie Dunes was five miles northeast of Hutchinson. Paved roads stopped two miles west of the entrance to the course. In 1935 there were only sand trails leading to the tract of land Perry Maxwell chose for the site of his masterpiece.

"These were roads we wouldn't drive our cars on today," said Claude Morris, one of the foremen on the original construction project. In 2002, at the grand age of 88, Morris was still living west of Hutchinson.

Morris recalled that in those days Kansas was rife with soap plants, thorny plum thickets, and prairie rattlesnakes. Of course, he said, "We were not supposed to talk about the snakes." Once the greens were built, the snakes would crawl on them to sun themselves and Morris had his crew rake them off with bamboo poles, kill them and bury them.

Charles Craig, head pro at Prairie Dunes for 31 years, said he has not seen a rattlesnake since he came in 1968. He said members brought in bull snakes, which are natural enemies of rattlesnakes. Apparently the bull snakes did their job.

The construction of the course was done with teams of horses and mules, 18 in all, and slips and Fresno scrapers and wheelbarrows. There was not one piece of mechanized equipment except for the Model T and Model A Fords and trucks which took the workers to the site. The greens and fairways were cleared and scraped by teams dragging plows and scoops. The roots of native grass and weeds were all removed by hand, one wheelbarrowful at a time.

Morris said he had a crew of 43 men who worked on the greens. The crew was hired by the Works Progress Administration of Franklin D. Roosevelt's New Deal admin-

From the *Hutchinson News:*
With a list of prospective members already in his desk drawer, Emerson Carey, Jr., president of the Prairie Dunes Improvement Co., and former Kansas golf champion, today admitted he was itching to try the new sandhills links.

Outlining construction of the nine-hole course in the washboard contours of a 420-acre expanse four miles east of 30th and Main Sts., which Perry D. Maxwell, Ardmore, Okla., links architect declared was the finest natural topography for a golf course he has ever seen, Carey today said the facilities would not be ready until next September.

SECOND TO NONE

Maxwell was in Hutchinson this week to trace construction progress. Builder of the beautiful Ledger course in Philadelphia, the swanky Twin Hills links at Oklahoma City and picturesque course at the University of Michigan, he told Carey the near-Hutchinson course would be second to none in the country.

Like many famous courses, Prairie Dunes will have no water hazards.

There will be no dearth of water for greens, trees and fairways, however, Carey declared, reporting the water system comprising five 100-foot wells and between 12,000 and 13,000 feet of pipes was completed.

Most of the water lines have been constructed of "transite," mixture of 85 percent cement and 15 percent asbestos. They range in size from two-inch to eight-inch. Smaller pipes are of galvanized iron and copper.

COVERS 100 ACRES

The course itself covers approximately 100 acres of the tract of land. Nearly a dozen men were busy today grading greens, preparatory to planting.

A garage, shop and tool shed are nearly completed, and Curtis Peugh, contractor, has begun construction of the greenkeeper's house, to be a five-room cottage.

Erection of the clubhouse has not yet begun.

USE NATURE'S HANDIWORK

Chief construction problem of other golf courses has been entirely lacking here. Erection of billows of earth, excavation of traps and bunkers and formation of new landmarks has been achieved over a period of centuries by the master architect, nature. Wind, not modern power shovels, eroded valleys and piled up hummocks of sand, now laced into place by roots of wild plums and other shrubbery.

The rough will be very rough.

Fairways will be perfect as Maxwell's proven ingenuity can make them, Carey promised.

EASY TO GET MEMBERS

As for membership in the club he heads, Carey declared: "I won't have any trouble getting the 110 players the club will be limited to. It will probably be a bigger problem turning down the surplus."

He still wishes it were not so long until he can stride onto the course, tee his ball, swing a driver and feel the impact of the club against sphere, sending the pellet whistling down a perfect fairway between some of nature's "roughest rough."

istration. Another WPA crew built the fairways.

Hole No. 2, which is considered a natural beauty, was carved out of the side of the tallest dune on the course. The crew dug a hole in the side of the dune and leveled the dirt to make the green. The excavation also created a large bunker behind the green, one of five bunkers that surround the green today.

Morris said the excavation came in handy one day when one of those tornadoes for which Kansas is famous came whirling past, west of the dune. "I got most of the men down into that hole we had dug," he said. "I figured that was the safest place."

The green that caused the biggest problem, said Morris, was No. 8, which today is hailed as one of the course's finest and most treacherous. The green sat near the top of a tall dune where it was unprotected from the wind and was consistently drying out. Morris sent one of the older WPA workers up the hill with orders to keep the green dampened down. That was his only job. He did it every day for almost

Construction campsite west of present-day No. 11 tee. (Prairie Dunes)

a month until the grass rooted and took a firm stand.

The topsoil that was used came from the bunkers, and from two other sources that left landmarks that remain features of the course today. Part of the soil came from a lake that was dug north of the No. 7 (now No. 10) green and from a borrow pit near today's No. 14 green. The lake is kept filled by five water wells and is used only for irrigation.

The man who directed the project was Dean Woods, Maxwell's construction engineer and brother-in-law. Woods was a former semipro baseball player with big, gnarly hands, according to Dora Harrison, Maxwell's daughter. He was as important to the Prairie Dunes project as Perry Maxwell was to Alister MacKenzie's much celebrated courses in Michigan—Crystal Downs and the University of Michigan.

Pointing up the importance of Woods's contribution to the creation of Prairie Dunes is the fact that in building the greens Morris dealt only with Woods. Maxwell would undoubtedly drop in from time to time, but Morris said, "I never laid eyes on Perry Maxwell. I have no idea what he looked like."

Woods was the engineer on most of Maxwell's projects in the 1920s and 1930s. He was credited by some with knowing

David Pauls and his Fresno scraper.
Both played a key role in the 1936 project. (Prairie Dunes)

Opposite page, top: Original entrance to Prairie Dunes. Note clubhouse at the top of the hill. (Prairie Dunes)

Opposite page, bottom: Early-day clubhouse. (Prairie Dunes)

Seven teams of 18 horses and mules moved all the earth in the construction. (Prairie Dunes)

as much about designing and building a green as Maxwell. Woods worked on almost all of Maxwell's Oklahoma courses, including Southern Hills. He also assisted at Crystal Downs in Franklin, Michigan.

Woods had an apartment in Hutchinson for two years while he completed the construction of Prairie Dunes. He always took up temporary residence at the site of the projects. His grandson, Bruzzi Westheimer Jr. of Ardmore, Oklahoma, said he remembers his grandmother telling of following her husband to the University of Michigan, to Pine Valley in New Jersey, to Augusta, Georgia, and to Fort Worth to carry out some of Maxwell's famous redesign plans.

His son-in-law, Jerry Westheimer Sr., said Woods worked for Maxwell until the early 1950s. Woods died in 1953 and thus did not get to see the 18 holes completed several years later.

There is an element of mystery in the planning of the additional nine holes in 1955-57. The club's history book, published in 1987, said Press followed Perry's routing plan for the additional nine holes. However Press told Ron Whitten, *Golf Digest*'s golf architecture editor, that he could never find his father's original routing.

That poses the question: Did Press conceive the addi-tional holes, or was he following a plan established by the elder Maxwell?

Charles Craig, Prairie Dunes club pro, said Everett Queen, the golf course superintendent at the time, showed him Perry Maxwell's original routing plan, which has since disappeared. A routing plan was printed in the *Hutchinson News Herald* June 12, 1955, that showed the progress of the work on Press Maxwell's addition. It shows the holes in basically the same layout as today but with considerable differences in length and configuration.

Morris recalled acting as flag man for Dean Woods while he surveyed Perry Maxwell's routing of the second nine holes. Woods took a transit and he and Morris spent several days trekking through the area where most of today's additional nine holes are located, north and northeast of the original nine.

However, Morris said they did not mark the spots for future construction. He also said they did not survey the area on the ridge where today's holes 3, 4, and 5 were added.

Jim Loveless, Prairie Dunes president in 1951, said Perry Maxwell's original plans were different from the eventual holes 3, 4, and 5. What today are holes 3 and 4 were to be

From the *Hutchinson News,* June 2, 1957:
Prairie Dunes Golf and Country Club unveils its new nine holes with a pro-amateur tournament starting at 10:30 a.m. Sunday.

Fourteen professionals, each competing with one amateur (most of them from home clubs) as a team of two, and with that player plus two from the Dunes as a team of four, will tour the course before it is opened to club members at about 2 p.m.

The public is welcome. Galleries may follow any of the competing foursomes.

New scorecards reveal the "regular course" covers 6,148 yards and has a par of 70, while the championship course covers 6,531 yards and has a par of 71.

STRETCH NO. 9

The par difference comes on Hole No. 9, which regularly covers 406 yards and has a par of 4, but in championship competition will be stretched to 473 yards and have a par of 5. Championship matches will be played from back tees, which in virtually every case are back from 12 to 30 yards from the regular tees, but with one exception, do not increase par.

Three new holes are now a part of the first nine. These are Nos. 3, 4 and 5. Six of the back nine holes are new. Old holes incorporated in the back nine are Nos. 10, 17 and 18.

The entire course is in excellent condition despite rains Friday night and Saturday morning. The new card:

| | FRONT NINE | |
No.	Dist.	Par
1	403	4
2	139	3
3	311	4
4	169	3
5	401	4
6	365	4
7	485	5
8	419	4
9	406	4
	3,098	35
CH.	3,319	36

one hole, and a par-3 hole was to be laid out to the north and west of the ridge behind today's No. 4 green.

Speculation is that combining holes 3 and 4 would have made one outstanding test of a par 4 that could have rivaled No. 8 as the course's signature hole. Loveless said that plan became impractical because there was a drainage problem in the location of the proposed par-3 hole. Because of the marshy conditions, it was never built.

Under the original concept, hole No. 5 would have been a long par 5 with a dogleg right, according to Craig. The tee would have been west of the dune, down from its present location, an area that would have been too wet, just as the proposed green for the original fourth would have been.

Jake Carey, charter member of the club and nephew of the founding Careys, agreed that combining today's holes 3 and 4 would have created another great hole. The drive would have been from an elevated tee to a fairway that doglegged sharply left to an elevated green with a bailout area on the left. It would have been an exacting par 4 with spectacular topography.

The setting was so good that, even divided, it provided a setting for today's holes 3 and 4 which complements Prairie Dunes' outstanding reputation.

By the time Press Maxwell was asked to design the additional nine holes, the era of slips and Fresnos pulled by mule and horse teams was long past. The construction of courses of that era involved bulldozers and considerable mechanized equipment.

The No. 4 green was dug out of the side of a sand dune much in the same manner that hole No. 2 was created in 1936. Part of a sand dune had to be knocked down to create the 12th hole. Several trees had to be grubbed out in the area of the 14th green and the 15th tee box. An old pit dump east of the 16th fairway was filled in (*Hutchinson News Herald*, June 12, 1955).

Over the years, the length of the holes has changed but only a few were altered materially. The course was lengthened by 206 yards between 1955 and 1964. Hole No. 5 was originally a 480-yard par 5 into the prevailing wind and No. 7 was a 440-yard, downwind par 4. Some time after 1955, No. 5 was shortened to 438 yards and 60 yards were added to No. 7 making it a par 5.

In the 1980s several championship tees were added, but only hole No. 12 was lengthened considerably, from 330 to

PRO-AMATEUR TOURNEY—*continued*

BACK NINE

No.	Dist.	Par
10	162	3
11	445	4
12	325	4
13	363	4
14	344	4
15	170	3
16	400	4
17	484	5
18	357	4
	3,050	35
CH.	3,212	35

Professionals in the pro-am contest will be in competition for more than $700 in cash prizes.

390 yards. It was proposed by Doug Petersan, superintendent at the time, who climbed atop a hill to the back and right of the existing tee with several key club members. What they saw was a spectacular setting with the fairway some 40 yards below, and creating a distinct angle change from the original tee. The hole that at one time was a 3-iron, 9-iron, became a driver or fairway wood and a short to medium iron second shot, elevated tee from atop the massive dune.

That is the only concession Prairie Dunes' keepers have made to the modern era. With today's advanced equipment, golfers are hitting the ball farther than ever. Prairie Dunes is so exacting it doesn't have to be extremely long, but it has added enough yards to keep the best of players honest.

Hole	1955	1964	2002	
1	415	436	432	
2	140	148	161	
3	330	326	355	
4	180	177	168	
5	480	436	438	*originally a par 5 into the south wind*
6	357	398	387	*new tee added in early 1980s*
7	440	501	512	*changed to par 5 after 1955*
8	395	424	430	
9	405	406	426	*new tee added in early 1980s*
	3,142	3,252	3,309	

Hole	1955	1964	2002	
10	170	170	185	*lengthened to its present yardage in early 1980s*
11	420	460	452	*lengthened from original design*
12	330	335	390	*elevated tee added in the 1980s*
13	380	409	395	*yardage added in early 1980s*
14	360	390	370	*new tee built in 1980s*
15	160	200	200	*present back tee added around 1980*
16	430	426	415	*additional championship tee added 1980s*
17	530	504	500	*originally a long par 5 into the south wind, shortened*
18	393	376	382	
	3,173	3,270	3,289	
Totals	6,315	6,522	6,598	
		+206	+76	

Chapter Four

❧ PRAIRIE DUNES ❧

When you first arrive at Prairie Dunes, it's as if Maxwell, the former small-town banker, is inviting you to step into a garden, to play a game without losing sight of the beauty of creation: the ups and downs of the smooth and gentle hills and dells, dunes and mounds, above old ocean beds of sand, with bones of birds and bison and Native Americans, wrapped with ribbons of green and fringed by waist-high prairie flora.

People look at Prairie Dunes and immediately look around for the sea. Here are the dunes but where is the water? It looks so like the rolling terrain that links the seacoast with the land. There is no other inland course like it.

". . . Prairie Dunes could be transported 'as is' from the

Entrance to Prairie Dunes Country Club.
(Prairie Dunes)

beautiful prairie to the coasts of the Irish Sea or the North Sea, where the roots of the game will always be, and it would be right at home," said Joe Dey, former executive director of the USGA, in the 1960s (*Prairie Dunes, the First 50 Years*, p. 88).

There is virtually no water on Prairie Dunes. It would require a horribly struck shot to moisten a ball in the only lake on the course, located in front of the 11th tee, whose primary purpose is to provide water for irrigation. It has no bearing on the strategy of playing the course.

Prairie Dunes is buried deep in the heartland of America, nestled in the south-central portion of Kansas. The only time this land was close to the sea was in the distant geological past.

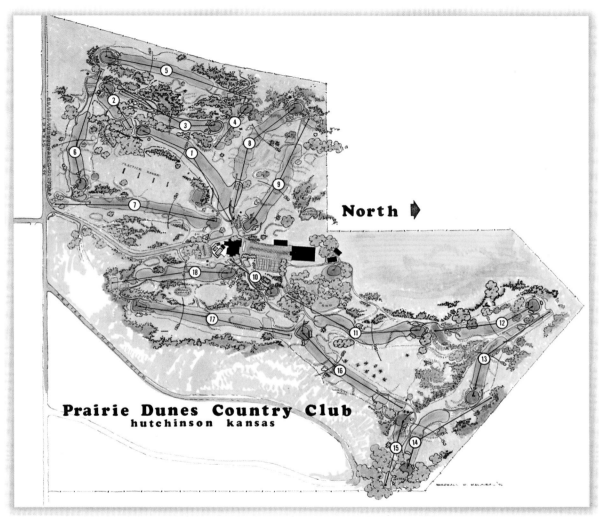

The present-day layout of Prairie Dunes. (Prairie Dunes)

The salt deposits and the sand dunes in Kansas were formed by the evaporation of Permian seas around 245 to 286 million years ago, according to geologists. The seas rose and fell in Kansas, covered the plains and dried up, leaving salt, gypsum, potash, and sand.

And it all just lay there for eons waiting for man to come along, particularly a man like Perry Maxwell, or men like those in the Carey family, to put it to good use.

The salt deposits extend from Nebraska through Kansas to northern Oklahoma. Salt mining became a major industry in Hutchinson, dominated by the Careys, a family that built a majority of the golf courses in the city from the turn of the twentieth century.

Although Hutchinson is landlocked, the seas were a strong influence on the use to which the land was put.

It was the ancient seas that formed the terrain and it was the influence of the Scottish seaside links that convinced William D. P. Carey that Hutchinson's sand dunes would be an ideal site for a golf course. He and brother June took action.

"They chose Perry Maxwell because of his familiarity with the Scottish links," said Jake Carey.

Maxwell was born in Princeton, Kentucky, but was descended from Scottish immigrants. Once he became interested in golf, he made a trip back to Scotland and familiarized himself with Scottish golf courses.

One more factor that contributes to a seaside atmosphere at Prairie Dunes is the wind, which constantly buffets the Scottish links and western Kansas as well. It was the wind whipping the sands around the Kansas prairie that created the dunes.

Western Kansas is among the windiest places in the United States. The National Oceanic and Atmospheric Administration rank Dodge City, just 120 miles west of Hutchinson, the second windiest city in the United States. Dodge City's mean wind speed is 13.9 miles per hour. That is "mean" speed for a 24-hour period, which includes the nighttime hours when wind dies down. The wind in western Kansas *normally* gusts 25 to 30 miles per hour and frequently reaches 40 to 50 mph. Some days it does not gust but blows in an unrelenting 15 to 20 miles per hour or more for entire days.

Kansas is an Indian word meaning "south wind." It is the land where cold fronts and warm fronts collide, where cold, dry air from the north meets sodden currents from the Gulf of Mexico, creating a "tornado alley."

The wind from the south and southwest is so strong and so nearly incessant that trees and bushes that are not shielded are permanently deformed, growing eerily bent to the north. Their leaning gives the impression that the wind is blowing a gale even during complete calm.

In the vast expanses of the Great Plains, as poet Robert Frost put it, "The only windbreak is the North Star."

This is a formidable challenge to golfers when aiming at Prairie Dunes' narrow fairways and small, undulating greens. The wind has been known to blow a golf ball off a green even after the ball has come to a complete stop. Attempting to stand steady in the wind over a putt on one of Maxwell's severely undulating greens can also give new meaning to the words "apprehension" and "yips."

Seaside wind is seldom more perplexing than the Kansas wind. When a Kansas golfer plays in other areas of the

A native grass that forms the
"gunsch" at Prairie Dunes.
(Zeke McCabe)

country, wind is seldom a problem. It is frequently faint or nonexistent. In competition, Kansas' golfers prefer wind. It gives them an advantage. If a player wants to play golf in calm conditions, they don't have much of an opportunity to do so at Prairie Dunes.

Another thing constantly in the back of the minds of golfers at Prairie Dunes is the "gunsch," a term applied to the growth of native grasses, plum thickets, yucca plants, soap weeds, and various other flora which thrive just off the fairways.

Prairie Dunes' gunsch makes the "rough" at other courses seem downright inviting. The gunsch lies there waiting to ingest errant golf balls. It is frequently impossible to find balls hit into the Prairie Dunes rough. Golf clubs have been lost in the gunsch. Even if you are able to locate the ball, hitting it out of the tangled growth can be a Herculean task.

So the wind and the gunsch can temper the boldness of the big hitter and cause even the most macho of golfers to reach for an iron off the tee instead of a wood. It is seldom profitable to challenge Prairie Dunes, yet if you hit the good shot, you are not penalized.

In the beginning, Prairie Dunes bore an even more striking resemblance to the Scottish links than it does today. There were virtually no trees when the course was first built. Many trees have invaded the course, mostly mature cottonwoods. Their presence only changes the appearance of the course, hardly ever the strategy needed to play it.

Trees encircle the back of the green at No. 14 but do not hinder the approach. At hole No. 15, the tee shot is directed between two trees. But only on hole No. 12 do trees come prominently into play. They stand sentinel in front of the 12th green. But trees do not line the fairways as they do on many other U.S. courses.

On at least five holes, the Maxwells tempt the long drivers to take shortcuts or to try to reach the green in less than the regulation number of strokes, but woe to the player who tries a shortcut and hits a poor shot.

"Prairie Dunes is the kind of course we should study," says

A native grass that forms the "gunsch" at Prairie Dunes.
(Zeke McCabe)

Ben Crenshaw. "With this new technology everybody hits the ball so far, but [at Prairie Dunes] you have to hit it remarkably well. The rough has always been a key part of Prairie Dunes."

Crenshaw pointed to a Maxwell maxim as the key: "If you pick a suitable piece of ground and make your holes fit your land-scape, your golf course will be different than anybody else's."

There was never a better example of that than Prairie Dunes.

Crenshaw and partner Bill Coore were engaged to rework the first two greens at Prairie Dunes in 1986. Crenshaw said Doug Petersan, the golf course superintendent at the time, needed more cupping locations.

Petersan said the primary reason for rebuilding the greens was that there were spots on the first and second holes where the ground was sinking and water was left standing. He said that the soil dredged up in the original construction in that area had more clay and less sandy loam and did not stand up as well as the rest of the greens, all but one of which are in their original conformation.

Crenshaw said he has such great respect for Maxwell's ability to design a green that he changed it as little as possible. Crenshaw told Perry Maxwell's daughter Dora that he and his partner think Maxwell "hung the moon." As a result, he modified the greens with great caution.

"I tried to soften the undulations of the greens slightly," said Crenshaw.

Maxwell's greens are noted for their severity. They were known as the "Maxwell Rolls," a play on the names of two luxury automobiles popular in the 1930s, the Rolls Royce and the Maxwell, made famous by comedian Jack Benny. A touch of irony is the fact that Maxwell actually drove a Maxwell automobile. His daughter, Dora Harrison, attests to that fact.

The greens were considered severe even in the 1930s, when grasses and technology were not able to create slick

A native grass that forms the "gunsch" at Prairie Dunes. (Zeke McCabe)

conditions common today. Today they are more treacherous than ever because modern equipment makes the surfaces of the greens slicker and faster. Sometimes it is difficult to keep the ball on one of Maxwell's greens.

Prairie Dunes is not a long course, which is also typical of Maxwell's designs. Prairie Dunes measures 6,598 yards, while some modern-day monstrosities exceed 7,400 yards.

The fairways are narrow, between 29 and 38 yards. The average width is 30 yards, compared to 40 to 60 yards for many modern courses. Old-timers say the Prairie Dunes fairways at one time were even narrower.

Moderate length is also typical of many older courses which have been judged superior to most modern courses. In *Golf Digest's* 2001 ranking of the top 100 U.S. courses, there were only two among the top 30 that were built after the 1930s. *Golf Magazine's* top 100 list included five from the post-World War II era among the top 30.

Among *Golf Magazine's* top 100 U.S. courses, Prairie Dunes was No. 13 and Southern Hills was No. 26. In *Golf Magazine's* world rankings, Prairie Dunes ranked No. 21 and Southern Hills No. 44. Prairie Dunes was No. 26 on *Golf Digest's* list of top 100 U.S. courses and Southern Hills was 15th.

"Maxwell's courses were so well bunkered, and the rough has always been a key part," says Crenshaw. "That keeps you so honest. And trying to putt those greens is an exacting task. A tough course doesn't have to be 7,400 yards."

Perhaps the highest praise Maxwell's courses have received was when they were selected in back-to-back years for the USGA's two biggest events—Southern Hills for the 2001 U.S. Open and Prairie Dunes for the 2002 U.S. Women's Open.

The 2002 U.S. Women's Open Championship is the first major professional event contested at Prairie Dunes, but many outstanding players had already tested the course. Three U.S. Women's Amateur tournaments, the 1986 Curtis Cup competition (team matches between the United States and Great Britain-Ireland) and other USGA national amateur and regional events have previously been staged there.

Hutchinson is a city of some 40,000 people. Fifty miles

to the southeast is Wichita, a city of 300,000 with a metropolitan market area of barely half a million. If Prairie Dunes were located in a more heavily populated area, it undoubtedly would have been the site of several major events.

"Anyone who thinks he has seen all the distinctive American courses is mistaken if he has not yet seen Prairie Dunes," said Frank Hannigan, then assistant director of the USGA, in 1964. "If the course were situated near a large urban center, it would surely be one of the most celebrated in the country."

Maxwell's desire for the least disruption of nature is being observed in other ways at Prairie Dunes. The course has become a wildlife and habitat management preserve under Audubon International.

More than 100 acres of undisturbed prairie encircle the course and 75 acres of prairie habitat are maintained through the golf course. Prairie Dunes participated in the 1997 Bird Watching Ryder Cup and there were 47 species identified during the 24-hour event.

Maxwell maintained that retaining natural features paid off in low maintenance costs. That has proved to be true at Prairie Dunes.

The average life of a green is 20 to 30 years. Yet seven of the nine original greens are still in use at Prairie Dunes after 65 years. The additional nine holes are now 45 years old and only one of those has been rebuilt.

The reason for this, in the opinion of Stan George, the current golf course superintendent, is that the soil that was

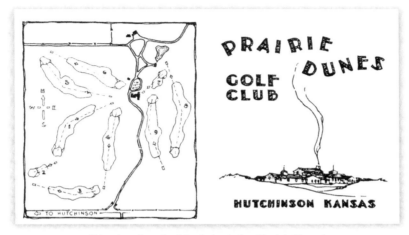

Line drawing of original nine holes. (Prairie Dunes)

Wilson served from 1937 until he retired in 1970. His assistant, Charles Craig, took over in 1970 and is still the head pro.

George is only the fifth golf course superintendent in the same span. Previous superintendents include Petersan and Red Lambert, former president of the Golf Course Superintendents Association of America.

pushed up in making the greens was sandy loam similar to that used in the refurbishing of greens. Also, Maxwell's severe rolls allow for excellent drainage.

Prairie Dunes also has low maintenance costs because 75% of the 240 acres the course occupies remains in its native state.

Stability has been the key to the golf staff. Prairie Dunes has had only two head professionals in its 65 years. Ross

Petersan is a nationally prominent superintendent credited with pulling off one of the most successful renovations in the nation at Baltimore Country Club's East Course, an A. W. Tillinghast design.

Petersan went to Baltimore Country Club in 1991 when he left Prairie Dunes. He is now the superintendent at the Austin, Texas, Golf Club, a Ben Crenshaw-Bill Coore design which opened in 2000.

❦ The Old Course ❧

On September 3, 1937, ten days before the official opening, William and June Carey joined club pro Ross Wilson and Dean Woods, Perry Maxwell's construction engineer, in the first foursome to play Prairie Dunes.

At the time, the course measured only 3,165 yards and carried a par of 35 for men, 39 for women. They toured the layout twice. Wilson had the best score of 35-41=76, six over par. June Carey shot 83, Bill Carey 86, and Woods 93.

The account of the match said that the Carey brothers intended to increase the layout to 18 holes in the near future and add another 18 holes later (The *Hutchinson News*, Sept. 4, 1937).

Because of World War II and other factors, it would be 20 years before the additional nine would be built. The second 18 never came to pass.

For the first three years the course remained in perfect condition, according to a story in the *Hutchinson News* of June 12, 1955. In 1940, a heavy freeze killed most of the Bermudagrass on the fairways. Still later, standing water killed huge patches of fairway grass.

In December 1941, just four years after the completion of the course, the bombing of Pearl Harbor ushered the United States into World War II. Activity at most golf courses came to a virtual standstill. Courses could not be properly maintained because gasoline, machinery, and man-

Hole	Yards	Men's Par	Women's Par
1	415	4	5
2	140	3	3
3	335	4	4
4	440	4	5
5	395	4	5
6	400	4	5
7	160	3	3
8	510	5	5
9	370	4	4
Totals	**3,165**	**35**	**39**

❦ Original Configuration ❧

power were needed in the war effort. Golf balls were at a premium because all rubber also went to the war effort.

Only the healthiest golf course operations survived the war. Many courses were grown over and never reclaimed.

Prairie Dunes was apparently never in danger. The members' efforts were augmented by the presence of a nearby naval air training base, which provided added support because the officers enjoyed playing golf.

Perry Maxwell's original layout was a thorough test of golfing skills even though it included only nine holes. Those nine were the present-day 1, 2, 6, 7, 8, 9, 10, 17, and 18, with a par of 35.

Today, those same holes would be an even stiffer test. The original nine holes as configured today measure 3,415 yards from the back tees, 250 yards longer than in the beginning, and with a par of 36 instead of 35 (today's No. 7, then No. 4, was originally a par 4 of 440 yards). The greens would also be significantly faster and more difficult.

Holes 1 and 6 required the golfer to work the ball from right to left and holes 8, 17, and 18 required working it left to right. In its original configuration, today's No. 2 and No. 10 (then No. 2 and No. 7) were the par 3s and today's No. 17

(then No. 8) was the lone par 5.

Holes 2, 8, 10, and 17 are the most celebrated holes on the course. They were the original 2, 5, 7, and 8.

Three of them are among the top 100 holes in the United States as determined by a panel of experts polled by *Golf Magazine*. They are Nos. 2, 8, and 10. No. 17 was also rated as one of the nation's best short par 5s (500 yards or less).

This leaves little doubt as to why many considered it the best nine-hole course in America during its first 20 years of existence. The man most insistent that it was the nation's best nine was Johnny Dawson of Chicago, a Walker Cupper who was an official of Spalding Sporting Goods, of which his brother was president.

A host of accomplished golfers, including Dawson and champions of Colorado, Oklahoma, Missouri, and Nebraska, were on hand for the official opening on September 13, 1937, including Fred Dold of Wichita, former Kansas state champion and eventual member of the USGA Executive Committee.

Dawson told a Hutchinson newspaper reporter he found the conformation of the greens "most interesting," the distances "deceptive," and the course a "true test of golfing skills."

Hole No. 2 in the early days. (Prairie Dunes)

Maxwell told the reporter, "I told you the boys would agree with me when I said there isn't another nine-hole course like it in the whole United States."

The second hole has been respected, feared, revered, and yes, intimidating, from the start for its natural beauty and for the strategy that it demands. It sits on a

A view from the south of the treacherous second green. (Prairie Dunes)

shelf built into the side of a huge dune surrounded by five bunkers. The prevailing wind from the left (as well as into the player's face) and the small green, make it difficult to judge which club to use. If you are short, you face a blind chip shot or have to hit out of a deep bunker. If you are long, you have to contend with another bunker or the course's famous gunsch on the side of the hill. Hit it to the right and there's more trouble—sand and deep native grasses.

The No. 2 green is the most difficult of the par-3 greens. The worst position is on the backside of the green because it is all downhill, both literally and figuratively.

Hole No. 8 is the most storied hole on the course, to the extent of almost being considered hallowed ground. It has been included among nearly every publication's list of the top-rated 100 holes in the world. It first got its due recognition in 1966 when *Sports Illustrated*'s Dan Jenkins, with input from the legendary Ben Hogan, picked it as the best eighth hole in America. Any errant shot that fails to hit the fairway will find severe trouble. On the left is the gunsch and on the right is gunsch plus a steep drop-off.

There is trouble lurking in the fairway because of severe

Member foursome plays hole No. 8 (circa 1941). (Prairie Dunes)

undulations and swales so deep that carts and tractors drop out of sight at the bottom of them. On this fairway the golfer more than likely will have an uneven stance, and perhaps even a blind shot to the green.

Once on the green, the troubles are far from being over. This is one of the most severe greens on the course.

Perry Maxwell loved elevated greens and elevated tees and used them wherever he could find them. On the original hole No.7 (now 10), he had both.

Perry Maxwell himself, normally a modest and conservative fellow, called this the best par-3 hole in America. The green is perched atop a hill 185 yards away. Missing the green in any direction leaves the player in trouble. There is nearby gunsch on three sides and bunkers at the left front and right front.

The key is club selection, complicated by a prevailing wind at the golfer's back. The distance is deceiving and it is all carry to a green that falls away from the player in the back portion of the putting surface.

Hole No. 8 (present-day No. 17) was originally even tougher than it is today. The original tee was farther west, close to the present-day No. 11 tee.

That created a severe dogleg right and made it a completely different hole than it is today. Jake Carey said he thinks the original was a better hole. Some may have gambled on a shortcut to the right but seldom was there a chance to go for the green in two shots.

Carey said he cannot remember any player trying to reach the green in two shots from the original tee, primarily because of the dogleg. "To cut off much of the distance you had to bite off a big hunk of deep rough," he said.

He said he wishes that Press Maxwell had made a double tee for 11 and 17 and left the 17th hole in its original configuration. Today the hole is shorter and almost straightaway.

To Press Maxwell's credit, however, today's 17th hole gives the better player a choice. The long hitter is tempted to try to reach the green with the second shot. This option adds drama and excitement for the good player. It is still a gamble, providing the player an opportunity to score anywhere from an eagle three to a double bogey seven. The 17th green is one of the two smallest on the course, and one of the most difficult, having three distinctive tiers to challenge any player.

Also on the old course, hole No. 4 (now No. 7) was a long

Action on the original 7th green, (circa 1940). (Prairie Dunes)

❧ The Scorecard Today ❧

Hole	Yards			Men's	Women's
	Back	Middle	Front	Par	Par
1	432	401	390	4	4
2	161	142	138	3	3
3	355	308	272	4	4
4	168	150	134	3	3
5	438	402	391	4	5
6	387	360	324	4	4
7	512	487	429	5	5
8	430	417	359	4	4
9	426	400	320	4	4
Totals	3,309	3,067	2,757	35	36

Hole	Yards			Men's	Women's
	Back	Middle	Front	Par	Par
10	185	160	128	3	3
11	452	442	420	4	5
12	390	371	323	4	4
13	395	357	276	4	4
14	370	342	281	4	4
15	200	169	134	3	3
16	415	396	349	4	4
17	500	477	447	5	5
18	382	372	352	4	4
Totals	3,289	3,086	2,710	35	36
	6,598	6,153	5,467	70	72

par 4. Playing downwind made it easily reachable for many golfers. The better players could reach it in two shots even after the tee was moved back to add 71 yards and changed to a par 5. The bunkers at the two front corners of the green were extended to wrap around the front slightly, leaving a narrower opening.

All original holes except No. 7 and No. 17 are virtually unchanged from the way Perry Maxwell conceived them. An extra tee was built on No. 6. It added 52 yards but did not severely alter the character of the hole. What it did provide, however, was a splendid view of the hole from about 50 feet above the fairway.

A bunker was added at No. 2 and bunkers at other holes were expanded or reshaped and some fairway bunkers were built to keep balls out of the deep rough, yet the core components of the layout remain intact.

It is possible to get a feel for the original nine holes by playing them from the member tees. Yardages are almost identical to the original layout except on holes 7 and 17. The total yardage is 3,216 from today's member tees, compared with 3,165 for the original layout. Par, however, would be 36 because No. 7 is now a par 5 instead of a par 4.

{ THE ADDITIONAL NINE }

When he added nine holes in 1957, J. Press Maxwell inserted current holes 3, 4, and 5 into the front nine, and used holes 7, 8, and 9 as the new holes 10, 17, and 18.

Hole No. 3 was originally conceived as a long par 4 with an acute left dogleg to an elevated green on the side of a dune. A par-3 hole was to have been built west of the dune. Drainage problems could not be solved and the par-3 hole was scrapped. The terrain for the long par 4 was divided into a short par-4 hole and a par 3 similar to hole No. 2, but playing to the northwest instead of southwest.

Hole No. 3 has been lengthened from 330 yards to 355 by building a back tee on top of the dune. Hole No. 4 was originally a 180-yard, par 3 that was shortened to 168 yards.

A routing plan printed in the *Hutchinson News Herald* on June 12, 1955, also showed that hole No. 5 was originally a 480-yard layout with a dogleg left. That is par-5 length. However, it was shortened to 438 yards and at that length it is a difficult par 4 because it plays into a prevailing south wind.

Hole No. 11 is one of Press Maxwell's finest. It was conceived as a 420-yard hole but became the course's longest par 4 at 452 yards. Part of a sand dune had to be knocked down to create the new tee on the 12th hole, which also grew from 330 to 390 yards in the early 1980s.

Hole No. 17 not only was changed from Perry Maxwell's original concept but also from what Press Maxwell had envisioned. It originally was 510 yards long with a severe dogleg right. Press needed the original tee box for hole No. 11 so he moved the 17th tee east, removing the dogleg. It was to be 530 yards long, playing into the prevailing wind, but was shortened to 500 yards. At that distance it is still ranked as a difficult par 5 because of its small humpbacked green and its difficult greenside bunkering.

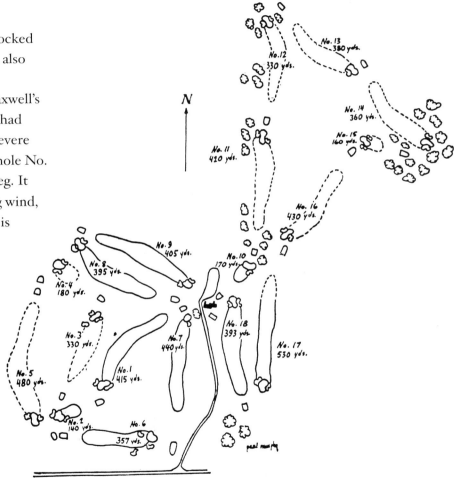

Line drawing of progress of Prairie Dunes expansion printed in the June 12, 1955, Hutchinson News. *Note the new holes have dotted lines for identification.*
(Hutchinson News)

❧ PRAIRIE DUNES PROGRESS REPORT ❧

From the *Hutchinson News*, June 12, 1955:
The new nine hole golf layout at Prairie Dunes Golf and Country Club is beginning to "take shape" and the original "nine" has never been in better condition.

This was the gist of a "progress report" on the Dunes Saturday, where members hope to have a completed 18 hole course second to none in the midwest, by about this time a year from now.

Work hasn't started on the air conditioning of the clubhouse—but no air conditioning has been needed. The heat was still on at the Dunes Saturday.

Press Maxwell, course architect, was here during part of the past week to oversee bulldozing work on the course.

In the accompanying map, broken lines indicate new holes and show where, at completion, one nine hole section will be south and west of the club-house, and the other north and east. No work has been done yet on holes No. 3, 4 and 5, which will tie with six of the present holes to form the front line.

Here is what has been done on the "back nine."

No. 11—Fairway has been leveled and the green "roughed in."

No. 12—Part of a sand dune has been knocked down, the fairway graded, tee and green "roughed in."

No. 13—Fairway has been graded, and a drainage ditch dug to take care of a potential "water problem." Green has been shaped, roughly.

No. 14—Several trees have been grubbed out to

open area for green and green approach.

No. 15—Trees have been grubbed out at site where tee will be located.

No. 16—An old pit "dump" east of the fairway has been filled in. Fairway has been brought to a rough grade.

Pipe for irrigating new fairways and greens is expected in mid-July. Meantime ditches are being dug for the pipe. Present reservoir and pump system are considered adequate for additional irrigation

which will be necessary.

The Prairie Dunes golf course was first opened in 1937, and it stayed in perfect condition for about three years. Then a heavy freeze killed out most of the Bermuda on the fairways. Still later standing water killed huge patches of fairway grass.

The water drainage problem apparently was solved two years ago.

Acres of fairway were replanted with Bermuda stolons, and this year, following recent rains, the course seemingly has regained its early perfection.

Chapter Five

{ MAXWELL'S ROLLS }

Maxwell's rolls are famous the world over. The severe undulations Perry and Press Maxwell built into their greens are typical of the hallowed designs of the old masters he followed such as Alister MacKenzie, Donald Ross, and A. W. Tillinghast. It was Perry Maxwell's redesign of the greens at Augusta National, Colonial Country Club in Fort Worth, and Pine Valley that played a major role in earning him his enviable reputation.

Prairie Dunes is admired for its natural setting, but there is general agreement that what sets it apart are Maxwell's greens.

At Prairie Dunes, the greens have been kept safe from the encroachment of the concept of greater and greater green speeds. But such legendary greens are coming under pressure at other clubs.

The green speed craze is not the first threat to maintaining the character of Maxwell's original greens. The greens at Maxwell's first creation, Dornick Hills Country Club in Ardmore, Oklahoma, were rebuilt long before the speed craze at the request of members who wanted the severity reduced, causing one pro golfer to remark that "Maxwell is probably spinning in his grave."

Over the years, some architectural firms have rebuilt some of the old Perry Maxwell greens in Oklahoma to soften the undulations. In Colorado, Press Maxwell built some 18 courses with the typical severe rolls, and these are being modified, too. This does not sit well with purists.

On the other hand, some clubs have lamented the gradual loss of definition of Maxwell greens. As a result, several architects have landed important jobs restoring the greens to their original design on courses in Oklahoma, including Southern Hills Country Club. The Southern Hills restoration work went to Keith Foster of Lexington, Kentucky, and was done in advance of the 2001 U.S. Open. He also restored some of Maxwell's work at Colonial Country Club.

An example of the Maxwell "Rolls" on the treacherous 17th green. (Stan George)

"It's scary," said Foster of the pressure being brought to bear on the old masters. "It's a terrifying thing. No one is defending the classic old courses."

Even though many of the old courses are among the most revered of those from the golden era of golf, the demand for greater green speeds has been difficult to satisfy. Foster said all of the older courses have two or three greens that would be marginally unfair at speeds of 10.5 and faster. Among them would be holes 9 and 18 at Southern Hills and 2, 8, and 17 at Prairie Dunes.

The job of restoring Maxwell greens at two Oklahoma country clubs in Muskogee and Lawton was awarded to Tripp Davis and Associates of Norman, Oklahoma.

"The game of golf is tradition," Davis said. "I would fight hard to keep the old traditional greens and I think the clubs that have those great old courses are smart enough to do that. They understand what they've got and that there is a definite need to keep the greens at a slower speed to be playable."

Davis pointed out that clubs and equipment are developing to the point where it is necessary to keep adding length to courses to maintain standards. "But the greens are where par can be preserved," he said. "Speeds of 9 and 10 on a green that is smooth and fast, that's as fast as you need to get for members."

Davis said in preparing to restore the greens in Muskogee and Lawton, he did not have photographs or charts to help visualize the original greens. So he went to Prairie Dunes, Crystal Downs, Saucon Valley, the National Golf Links, and Pecan Valley in San Antonio to study Maxwell's designs. Then he rebuilt the greens with those courses in mind.

Cutting the grass short enough to attain speeds of 10 to 12 feet threatens the health of the typical grasses used on greens. The shorter the grass is cut the more difficult it is for the golf course superintendent to keep it growing. This has been a major concern of the Golf Course Superintendents Association of America.

A Stimpmeter measures the speed of greens. Edward S. Stimpson invented the device in 1936 but the USGA did not adopt its use until 1978. A Stimpmeter is a 3-foot metal trough with an indentation on one end. A golf ball is laid into the indentation and the trough is raised until the ball rolls out. The number of feet the ball rolls is used to gauge the speed of the green.

Stimpson did not design his meter in order to emphasize

speed, but to create uniformity in green speeds as an aid to the golfer. The concept of green speed, however, has grown out of control, with speeds at many places now in excess of 11 feet on the Stimpmeter.

Today's maintenance equipment can mow grass short enough for Stimpmeter readings up to 13 feet. In the 1930s maintenance equipment could not create anything faster than 6 or 7. That was the speed Maxwell and the early-day architects targeted in creating their designs. As late as 1976, when the USGA did its first testing with the Stimpmeter, the average speed of greens was still between 6 and 7 feet. That speed grew with the advent of better mowing equipment, double-cutting practices, and use of rolling machines to make the green even faster.

The idea of 12-foot green speeds at Prairie Dunes is unrealistic. At Prairie Dunes, finding 10 level feet of turf on any of the greens is difficult. So Stimpmeter tests were out of the question except on one or two greens until recently, when researcher Douglas Brede came up with a formula for calculating the speed of a sloped green.

Just how demanding Prairie Dunes' greens are is brought home by the fact that the Stimpmeter is the subject of

Prairie Dunes humor. The mere mention of one brings a chuckle to Prairie Dunes club pro Charles Craig.

Stan George, the current Prairie Dunes golf course superintendent, said he seldom uses his Stimpmeter for the purpose to which it was intended. He uses it mostly as a small shovel to dig troughs to drain water off low spots on tees. Doug Petersan, the previous superintendent, once joked that he should have his Stimpmeter bent into a circle and see how far it would roll.

As the greens became faster and faster, Maxwell's greens became more and more treacherous. Green speeds of higher than 10 on Maxwell's layouts are considered to be unfair. In several instances it is difficult to keep a ball on the green.

Prairie Dunes greens are small by today's design standards. The average green on the PGA Tour contains some 6,000 square feet. The typical green is more like 6,500 square feet and the size ranges all the way to 11,000 square feet. Greens at some modern courses average 10,000 square feet, according to PGA Tour statistics. The average green at Prairie Dunes is 4,279 square feet. The smallest greens are at holes No. 2 and 17. They measure 3,419 square feet. The largest is No. 15 at 4,899.

Cutting the grass to the height required in order to attain speeds of 10 feet or more not only endangers the turf but also reduces the number of acceptable hole locations, for which a minimum of three feet of level area in which to stop the ball is recommended. The smaller the green, the fewer acceptable hole locations. Fewer hole locations means the ground around the area is more compacted by traffic.

An architectural firm found that one of the Press Maxwell greens in Colorado had less than 26% of the surface area suitable for hole locations. Two or three greens at Prairie Dunes have an even smaller percentage area than that.

At Prairie Dunes the greens are cut to a speed of between 8 feet, 6 inches and 9 feet, 6 inches. George said most club members are happy with a 9-foot speed. That is also the fastest speed that will allow him to maintain a healthy turf. The club handles approximately 30,000 rounds a year. George has said that is not considered to be heavy traffic and a healthy turf can be maintained within that range.

The wind at Prairie Dunes is also a factor. The wind can blow the ball off a surface with a green speed greater than 10 feet, 6 inches. "It's almost like glass," said Foster.

The USGA, in its Course Rating System evaluation, has set national guidelines for green speeds. Speeds of 8 feet, 6 inches and faster are deemed fast. Medium speeds are those between 7 feet, 6 inches and 8 feet, 6 inches. Slow greens are those less than 7 feet, 6 inches.

For tournament competition, fast speeds are those over 9 feet, 6 inches. Medium is 8-6 to 9-6 and slow is less than 8-6. Usually, the faster speeds are used only for major competition, which lasts for a week but also have to be maintained at that level for about a week prior to the actual event. Maintenance crews have a chance after that short period of stress to help grasses recover.

New grasses are being bred for higher speeds. An ultra-dwarf Bermuda is a strain that "requires" being cut to 1/8th inch height in order to remain healthy. The use of this grass on a Maxwell green would make it an "unfair" putting surface. Also, keeping the new grasses healthy is labor intensive.

Purists want the greens unaltered. The architects of the past weaved a magic into the way their greens received approach shots and in their demand that the golfer be able to read the green accurately in order to make the shot. The undulations also provide excellent drainage, which keeps the greens healthy.

Chapter Six

❦[THE FRONT NINE]❦

The front nine at Prairie Dunes is a blend of the old and the new. Press Maxwell did a masterful job of mixing his father's original design into his 18-hole concept.

The original nine holes surrounded the clubhouse. Holes 1 through 6 were on the west side of the clubhouse and holes 7, 8, and 9 were on the east. This was a cozy little concept. At no time was the golfer more than a couple of one-iron shots from the clubhouse.

When Press Maxwell completed his father's work, he produced the typical arrangement of two nines that go out from and back to the clubhouse.

In order to do this, he inserted three holes among the six original holes on the west, making the original 6th hole the 9th. Then he blended six other new holes in with the other three original holes to form the back nine.

This produced two nines of almost equal length and a good balance in the demand for golfing skills. The front nine contains the beautiful and natural second hole, the equally charming and more demanding eighth hole, and the difficult fifth hole, which was one of Press Maxwell's creations.

{ THE FIRST HOLE }
"Carey Lane"

PAR 4 | BACK: 432 | MIDDLE: 401 | FORWARD: 390

*"This usually plays back into the wind. It's a wonderful
starting hole. Maxwell raised both sides. You look at this and say,
'Here we go.' It's a hole kin to the British Isles."*
— BEN CRENSHAW

The drive is the key here and the ideal landing area is a difficult
target. It's a dogleg left into the prevailing southwest wind.
The ideal shot hugs the left side, but the visual of this shot is
deceptive as the player must try to calculate where the fairway
cuts back toward the green at the dogleg. The fairway narrows
considerably at about 140 yards from the green. If the player
allows the prevailing wind to push the ball to the right, he or
she could have trouble getting home in two shots. The green
is almost triangular in shape, narrower at the front. A very good
test for an opening hole and a par here is not easily made.

Crenshaw and partner Bill Coore reworked this green in
1986 to improve drainage.

No. 1 green (left) beside No. 2 tee, circa 1941. (Prairie Dunes)

Big hitters who let the prevailing wind push their ball to the right may have to contend with this bunker on the right side of the fairway. (John R. Johnson/golfphotos)

Hole No. 1, viewed from near the bunker on the right side of the green. (John R. Johnson/golfphotos)

Looking from behind the green back up the No. 1 fairway, a dogleg left. (Stan George)

{ THE SECOND HOLE }
"Willow"

PAR 3 | BACK: 161 | MIDDLE: 142 | FORWARD: 138

*"You get here and you just stare at it a while. It is bunkered so
well. The bunker in the back is pulled right out of the hill.
It is a very striking example of a natural setting. It plays into the
hillside at a slight angle. It's a magnificent green. A tough green;
exacting. It would never be dull. It is well thought out."*
— BEN CRENSHAW

The big problem here is club selection. If you are short, you
can have a 12-foot deep bunker shot. If you are long you can
be in another bunker or worse, in the gunsch behind the
green. The wind plays tricks here, too. Once you get on the
two-tiered green, your troubles are not over. It is one of the
smallest and most difficult greens on the course.

This hole is an ideal example of Maxwell's minimalist philosophy. It sits on a shelf on the side of the highest ridge on
the golf course.

Jerry Slack, Oklahoma golf architect who reworked a

Maxwell course in Coffeyville, Kansas, said when he saw
this hole, "I had a religious experience.

"There is no more picturesque hole anywhere. You have a
crosswind. There is no trouble on the left but the bunkers
are nasty and it's a tough green. If you try to turn the ball
over right to left and miss it's an easy bogey, but still fair."

Crenshaw and Coore also reworked this green in 1986.

The dune area prior to construction on hole No. 2. (Prairie Dunes)

*Opposite page: Hole No. 2, from the championship tee. There are five
bunkers, including one on the right behind the rough and another
behind the green. (John R. Johnson/golfphotos)*

Hole No. 2 from near the forward tee. The deep rough near the backside of the green creates the need for an exacting approach shot. The green is only 25 yards deep. (John R. Johnson/golfphotos)

Looking down on the No. 2 green from the top of the dune back toward the tee. (Prairie Dunes)

{ THE THIRD HOLE }
"Wild Plum"

PAR 4 | BACK: 355 | MIDDLE: 308 | FORWARD: 272

*"This is a short par 4. A lot of people club
down and try to hit a good second shot."*
—BEN CRENSHAW

This green beckons the big hitter. It is a short par 4 and the prevailing wind is at the golfer's back. But big trouble lurks on both the left and right. It is not a true dogleg but the elevated tee atop the highest point on the course is offset to the left so that the golfer is aiming at the fairway from an angle. The smart play is a layup, leaving the player a full wedge into the green. The green sits in a saddle on a ridge.

This is the first of three straight holes added to the front nine by Press Maxwell. A tee at the top of the ridge was built in the late 1980s, adding some 50 yards to the hole's original design.

Hole No. 3 seen from tee atop sand dune left of the fairway. (Prairie Dunes)

Two bunkers guard the front of the No. 3 green, creating a narrow opening. (John R. Johnson/golfphotos)

Early-day picture of hole No. 4 showing bunkers
and rough on three sides. (Prairie Dunes)

{ THE FOURTH HOLE }
"Hilltop"

PAR 3 | BACK: 168 | MIDDLE: 150 | FORWARD: 134

"This is a good par 3, bunkered tightly into the edge of the green."
—BEN CRENSHAW

At first glance this looks similar to hole No. 2 but it is completely different. The prevailing wind is still on the left but the tee shot is aimed 90° farther to the right, playing to the northwest. This green sits near the top of the hill and it typically plays one club longer than No. 2. There are sand bunkers short and long and a plum thicket on the right. It requires a cut shot. If the golfer is above the hole, he or she will have difficulty in getting down for par as the green slopes considerably from back to front.

There is a bailout area left of the green for the tee shot but it slopes severely to the left. A ball hit in this area will not find trouble but will roll down to the bottom of the hill and it requires a tricky chip shot.

A championship tee added 18 yards in the early 1980s.

There is a large bailout area on the left side of the No. 4 green but if the ball does not land near

the surface of the green it will roll back down the hill. (John R. Johnson/golfphotos)

❧ THE FIFTH HOLE ❧
"Quail Ridge"

PAR 4 | BACK: 438 | MIDDLE: 402 | FORWARD: 391

*"It plays longer than its yardage into the wind.
You can hit it out-of-bounds easily. This hole requires
a fine tee shot and a well-judged second shot."*
—BEN CRENSHAW

It appears there is not much trouble here, but the prevailing southwest wind blows into the side of the ridge on the left. You hit from an elevated tee to a fairway that slopes to the right. There is an out-of-bounds on the right, but there is plenty of open space.

The second shot is to an elevated green built into the side of a dune, and is protected by plum thickets and a large bunker. A massive bunker guards the front right of the green. The green itself also presents a challenge as there are plenty of subtle "rolls" on this green. Front right hole locations are the most difficult.

Opposite page: Looking from the fairway up to the elevated No. 5 green, which is long and narrow. (John R. Johnson/golfphotos)

Below: An early-day view of the fifth hole from the front bunker. (Prairie Dunes)

{ THE SIXTH HOLE }
"Cedar"

PAR 4 | BACK: 387 | MIDDLE: 360 | FORWARD: 324

"A beautiful hole. You can see all of it from the tee. The bunker on the left is so well placed that the hole runs around that beautifully."
—BEN CRENSHAW

Another of Maxwell's natural beauties. The layout sprawls on a rolling fairway that wraps around a bunker on the left side of the fairway. A sand bunker about 15 yards in front of the green creates that camouflage look that so many of the early great architects utilized, making the green appear to be sitting immediately behind the hazard.

This is another par 4 that issues a siren call to the macho hitter. One consolation is that the gluttonous gunsch is not close enough to be a serious problem for most golfers here. However, the high percentage approach shot is from the right side of the fairway, which does have a slope from right to left.

The area of the fairway bunker on the left is not the ideal spot for your drive to land on hole 6. (Prairie Dunes)

Opposite page: The foliage that populates the Prairie Dunes bunkers provides a foreground for a shot of the No. 6 green. (John R. Johnson/golfphotos)

Prairie Dunes' famous rough frames the landing area for hole No. 6. The hole should be approached from the right side of the fairway. (John R. Johnson/golfphotos)

The fairway bunker short of No. 6 green provides a problem in depth perception. (John R. Johnson/golfphotos)

{ THE SEVENTH HOLE }
"Southwind"

PAR 5 | BACK: 512 | MIDDLE: 487 | FORWARD: 429

*"With a helping breeze you can get there in two
but there is a tight entrance to the green. You can walk
off with a par or a six pretty easily."*
— BEN CRENSHAW

If it were not for this hole, one would hardly know there is a golf course upon arrival at the Prairie Dunes property. The fairway parallels the main drive to the clubhouse but is out of sight. Maxwell blended the other holes into the landscape so well they are not easily discerned.

There are two yawning bunkers on the right and left near the entrance to the green. The bunkers were in the original design but were expanded in the early 1980s to wrap around and protect the front of the green. This makes the approach more difficult than it was in its original form. It invites you to bump and run your approach shot but the narrow opening to the green requires an accurate shot.

View of the No. 7 green beside the No. 1 tee, before the bunkers were expanded to protect the entrance. (Prairie Dunes)

Opposite page: Hole No. 7 is a par 5, which is Prairie Dunes' most likely birdie hole. However, those trying to reach the green in two shots risk walking away with a six, or worse. (John R. Johnson/golfphotos)

{ THE EIGHTH HOLE }
"The Dunes"

PAR 4 | BACK: 430 | MIDDLE: 417 | FORWARD: 359

"This had to be one of Mr. Maxwell's favorite holes. It has a beautifully undulated fairway. Not only are you trying to hit it on line but also you seldom have a level lie. The green is on the side of a left-to-right slope and it is bunkered on the left side. You have a crosswind situation and another wonderful green."
— BEN CRENSHAW

This is the most heralded golf hole on the course. It has been ranked No. 9 among the top 10 holes in the United States and as the best No. 8 hole in a rating of the best 18 holes done by author Dan Jenkins and Ben Hogan in *Sports Illustrated* in 1966. It is a dogleg right uphill across a terrain that rolls like a tempest-tossed sea. By today's standards it is not extremely long and there is nothing bizarre about it. The troubles are subtle ones. Yet every shot must be precisely placed if the player is to have a good chance of making par.

The tee shot must be hit to the left side of the fairway, which doglegs to the right. The tee shot faces to the west, thus the player faces a wind that is both into and coming from the left of the tee. Hit through the fairway and the golfer is in some of the course's worst gunsch. On the right of the fairway are more deep native grasses, sometimes as high as two to three feet. The fairway slopes to the right and from that side of the fairway the player faces a blind shot to the green.

The second shot even from an ideal location is difficult to judge because it is uphill all the way and the fairway ripples like a washboard. If the player winds up in one of the swales that cross the fairway, they likely won't have a level stance. The green is so severely undulating that anything outside of 10 feet is a potential three-putt. Four-putting is not out of the question. If the hole is located on the front and the ball is on the back portion, the player faces a downhill and winding putt. And, oh yes, balls have been known to be putted off the green.

⋯⋯⋯⋯⋯⋯⋯⋯⋯⋯⋯⋯⋯⋯⋯⋯⋯⋯⋯⋯

Opposite page: Hole No. 8 from the top of the dune above the green. (Prairie Dunes)

Hole No. 8 is a dogleg right that wraps around deep rough and bunkers uphill to a well-bunkered green. (John R. Johnson/golfphotos)

Picking the correct club to reach the elevated green is only a part of the problem posed by hole No. 8. It is well protected by rough, bunkers, and a steep drop-off to the right and is one of Prairie Dunes' most difficult greens to read and putt. (John R. Johnson/golfphotos)

{ THE NINTH HOLE }
"Meadowlark"

PAR 4 | BACK: 426 | MIDDLE: 400 | FORWARD: 320

"This requires a good tee ball, and it has a low-profile green. It has a lot of interesting rolls to it. It is hard to guess the proper length on the second shot. My partner (Bill Coore) loves that hole. It's his favorite. He loves the green, it is so well bunkered."
— BEN CRENSHAW

Another rolling fairway that virtually assures that the player will not have a level stance for the second shot. The fairway runs from an elevated tee down into a vale and back uphill.

Even if the player is adept from the sand, he or she will want to avoid the bunkers. One has a yucca plant growing in it and others are lined with bushes.

This is another hole that poses a problem of correct club selection for the approach shot. The back tee was not a part of the original layout. It was added in the early 1980s at the top of the ridge behind No. 8 green and requires the player to aim between two trees.

Yucca plants and prairie grasses line the bunkers and frame the No. 9 green. (Prairie Dunes)

Opposite page: The typical bunker is a hazard, but Prairie Dunes' bunkers pose additional hazards – the yucca plants and other bushes that grow along the edge. (John R. Johnson/golfphotos)

Looking back down the fairway from No. 9 green, it is clear by the shadows cast on the rolling terrain that there is seldom a level lie for the golfer. (John R. Johnson/golfphotos)

Chapter Seven

❧ THE BACK NINE ❧

The back nine is an excellent blend of the designs of father and son. It begins with the spectacular par-3 10th hole, which was Perry Maxwell's pride and joy.

Immediately thereafter the golfer is faced with the demanding 11th, the most difficult of Press Maxwell's additions. It also begins a string of four holes, three of which are doglegs left.

Each hole presents the golfer with a different strategy to think his or her way through—wind direction, shot placement, club selection. Although the back nine lacks the undulations of the front nine except on the three original holes, it presents a greater variety of considerations and can be more exacting.

⟨ The Tenth Hole ⟩
"Yucca"

PAR 3 | BACK: 185 | MIDDLE: 160 | FORWARD: 128

"I have a picture of this hole taken about 1940.
I kept that picture because it is a beautiful hole. It is tree-lined
now and looks different. The green and bunkering make
it beautiful. The entrance is at the front left and there is a
bunker on the right. There are all sorts of problems."
—BEN CRENSHAW

A spectacular hole in every sense. One of the best green settings a golfer will find anywhere in the world. Golf course architect Jerry Slack of Broken Arrow, Oklahoma, said, "It's like trying to land your ball on an aircraft carrier downwind."

Club pro Charles Craig points out that the green is shallow (only 29 yards deep), considering the distance the ball must be hit. From the back tees it plays 25 yards longer today than when it was first designed because the tee was lengthened. Growth of trees on the left and gunsch in the rear make the target appear even smaller than it is.

The par-3 10th hole viewed from the forward tee. (Prairie Dunes)

Opposite page: The "gunsch" crowds up close around the bunkers
and the No. 10 green. (John R. Johnson/golfphotos)

{ THE ELEVENTH HOLE }
"Honey Locust"

PAR 4 | BACK: 452 | MIDDLE: 442 | FORWARD: 420

"A good two-shot hole. The mound in front
of the green is a nice feature."
— BEN CRENSHAW

This is the longest par-4 hole on the course. For most golfers it requires a long approach shot to the shallowest green. It is a dogleg left but there are no easy shortcuts. It is 260 yards of carry to the horseshoe-shaped bunker on the left side of the fairway and another 40 yards to the bend. The area between these two spots is the target area, and the ideal position is on the left side of the fairway.

Run-up shots are impractical because of a mound in the entrance to the green. The mound could divert a rolling ball into one of the two front bunkers. A ball that carries onto the front of the green will likely run clear through to the back fringe or, worse, the gunsch a few yards behind.

The horseshoe-shaped bunker at the bend in the dogleg left is just short of the ideal landing area for the tee shot on No. 11, which boasts a narrow fairway. A 290-yard tee shot leaves a 160-yard approach. (Prairie Dunes)

Opposite page: A 260-yard drive puts you beside the bunker on the left, but you are still 190 yards from the No. 11 green. (John R. Johnson/golfphotos)

The 11th green viewed from behind a cottonwood tree. (John R. Johnson/golfphotos)

Beware of the mound at the entrance to No. 11 green, which kicks running shots left or right. (John R. Johnson/golfphotos)

{ THE TWELFTH HOLE }
"Briar Patch"

PAR 4 | BACK: 390 | MIDDLE: 371 | FORWARD: 323

"The trees are the key here. A lot of people take out an iron on the tee. It does not pay at all to take on that tree [in the fairway]."
—BEN CRENSHAW

It is hard to imagine that this hole once was more difficult because of the presence of a large cottonwood tree on the left side of the fairway near the target landing area. The tree was damaged by lightning and had to be removed. However, there is still plenty of tree trouble. There are cottonwoods standing sentinel both left and right near the green, one of which sits in the fairway on the right about 90 yards short of the green. On the left are two other trees and a pair of bunkers. This leaves an extremely narrow opening to the green. A bump-and-run shot is frequently a necessity here to get under the tree.

This is the only hole where trees come into play prominently. Stay away from the back edge of the green, which slopes severely off toward the gunsch.

The elevated back tee was added in the early 1980s, and the high dune it sits on provides a stunning vista of much of the back nine layout.

An aerial view of Prairie Dunes' 11th, 12th, and 16th holes. (bottom)
(Zeke McCabe)

The original tee at No. 12 presented a dogleg left. A new elevated tee was added to the right and the hole was lengthened nearly 80 yards. (Prairie Dunes)

"39 Steps to Heaven" – From the 11th green to the back tee of No. 12 tee. (Zeke McCabe)

An aerial shot from behind the No. 12 green looking toward the 13th fairway. (Zeke McCabe)

The cottonwoods standing guard at No. 12 look even more ominous up close. (John R. Johnson/golfphotos)

{ THE THIRTEENTH HOLE }
"Sumac"

PAR 4 | BACK: 395 | MIDDLE: 357 | FORWARD: 276

"You feel off balance off the tee. It's a dogleg left and it's hard to put it down the left side and trust your shot."
— BEN CRENSHAW

P. J. Boatwright, former USGA executive director, took one look at the 13th green and said, "The only bad hole location on that green is where it is right now." (Meaning any hole location would be bad.) The hole sets up perfectly for a slight draw around a huge bunker perched on the left side of the dogleg.

There are also three fairway bunkers on the right, added in the mid-1980s because so many players slowed up play looking for their balls in the rough. These bunkers are situated in an area where it is possible to drive straight through the fairway and into trouble.

The green is slightly elevated and protected by front bunkers on the right and left. There is also a steep drop-off on the back right of the green, creating a touchy recovery shot in hopes of making par. The slight uphill second shot is misleading and usually requires one more club from the player to reach the green in regulation. Again, this green presents many subtleties and reading these is always difficult.

An aerial view of hole No. 13 from above the tee box. (Zeke McCabe)

Looking back down the fairway from above the No. 13 green. (John R. Johnson/golfphotos)

❧ THE FOURTEENTH HOLE ❧
"Cottonwood"

PAR 4 | BACK: 370 | MIDDLE: 342 | FORWARD: 281

"A good hole. You pick your poison off the tee. You have to carry the second shot all the way to the green."
—BEN CRENSHAW

To cut the corner on this dogleg left requires 260 yards of carry over rough, thickets, and a waste bunker 150 yards long on the left. The safe route, playing directly down the centerline of the fairway, leaves the player with a 160-yard approach shot. The green is narrow but 35 yards deep, with the back portion encircled by trees. It has a four-foot hump in the middle, creating a distinct separation from front to back. There are four bunkers and they all come into play.

An elevated back tee and the waste bunker were added in 1982 and 1983.

Towering cottonwood trees frame hole No. 14. (Prairie Dunes)

Opposite page: An aerial view of hole No. 14 and its huge waste bunker on the left. (Zeke McCabe)

An aerial view of the approach to the 14th green before the fairway bunker on the left was constructed. (Prairie Dunes)

The waste bunker on the left covers more than an acre of sand en route to No. 14 green, which is tucked into a grove of cottonwood trees. (John R. Johnson/golfphotos)

{ THE FIFTEENTH HOLE }
"The Chute"

PAR 3 | BACK: 200 | MIDDLE: 169 | FORWARD: 134

"This is a very difficult par 3. The tee is back quite a bit. There is usually a crosswind. It is a plateau green. Maxwell designed a lot of plateau greens. It takes an honest shot, but also the green drains very well."
— BEN CRENSHAW

The tee shot is through a narrow opening between two cottonwood trees. It is the longest par-3 hole on the course. There are two bunkers on the right of the green and deep gunsch close behind. The green is the largest on the course but still a modest 4,899 square feet. There is some room to the left of the green for a missed shot, but further left are deep plum thickets and out-of-bounds that can come into play.

Maintenance of this green has been complicated with the growth of volunteer trees and bushes. There is a dune on the south side of the green and the vegetation has hindered airflow to the green. This forced the maintenance crew to keep two large fans aimed at the green during the most humid and hottest parts of the summer. The trees and bushes are being cleared in order to resolve this problem.

Again, the green, as it is with most of the Maxwell greens, presents the golfer with a variety of putting experiences, most of which border on the extreme of being scary, due in part to the undulations as well as the speed.

Looking from behind the 15th green toward hole No. 14 with the No. 15 tee on the right. (John R. Johnson/golfphotos)

Cottonwoods frame the 15th green. The tee shot must be placed through the narrow opening at the "Chute" hole. (Prairie Dunes)

The narrow opening at No. 15 frames the par-3 green, which sits on the side of a sand dune. (John R. Johnson/golfphotos)

{ THE SIXTEENTH HOLE }
"Blue Stem"

PAR 4 | BACK: 415 | MIDDLE: 396 | FORWARD: 349

"A real good par 4 into the teeth of the wind. And it's all uphill."
—JERRY SLACK, GOLF COURSE ARCHITECT

This hole has two back tees, with the newest one located to the right of the original championship tee. It does not add yardage but it presents the golfer with a slightly different approach to the fairway from an angle and makes the dogleg right hole slightly more severe. It was added in 1987.

There are fairway bunkers right and left at the bend, 300 yards from the tee. This must be negotiated into the prevailing southwest wind. The green is narrow and the green is one of the deepest on the course. There are front bunkers left and right and the famous Prairie Dunes gunsch closes in on the player from the left.

Many golfers consider this, along with the ninth, to be one of the most underrated holes on the course.

From the landing area, hole No. 16 displays its hazards of bunkers and rough. (John R. Johnson/golfphotos)

The deepest (38 yards) green on the course awaits the golfer at hole No. 16. (John R. Johnson/golfphotos)

{ THE SEVENTEENTH HOLE }
"Pheasant Hollow"

PAR 5 | BACK: 500 | MIDDLE: 477 | FORWARD: 447

*"This green has confounded a lot of people. It's a lot of fun to play.
It plays back into the wind. It tempts a lot of people, which is
the mark of a good hole. Big hitters try to get there in two,
but the second asks for a really well-played shot. You may get
away with it one day and the next day you walk off with a 7.
If you don't go for it, it is a difficult pitch no matter where they
put the pin. It has the power to dictate play back toward the
tee box, and it's always tough putting across a convex green."*
— BEN CRENSHAW

This narrow fairway runs down a valley between two long dunes. The green is the most dangerous on the course. It is hogbacked and there is trouble close at hand on all sides — gunsch and bunkers on the left and a steep drop-off to the right. Hitting the small green is difficult, too, because of the wind and the terrain.

Just hitting the green is no guarantee of par. The green is narrow throughout, but is no more than 25 to 30 feet wide at the front. It is one of the two smallest greens on the course at 3,419 square feet.

The hole designed by Perry Maxwell was slightly different than it is today. Maxwell originally had the hole playing as a dogleg right, teeing off east of where the present No. 11 tee sits. The original hole was longer and could entice the longer hitter to cut the dogleg in an effort to go for the green in two. The more logical, and wiser, choice was to simply play directly down the fairway, lay up on the second and leave a short iron to the green. When the additional nine holes were built, that location was needed for the No. 11 tee. The tee today provides a fairly straightaway drive for the player, but the fairway does slide slightly left to right, creating opportunities for tee shots to move into the right rough. The old tee made No. 17 more difficult but did not provide the excitement of presenting the player the option of trying to reach the green in two shots.

• •

Opposite page: The most difficult green on a course famous for Perry Maxwell's demanding rolling surfaces awaits at hole No. 17. (John R. Johnson/golfphotos)

A deep bunker sporting yuccas and tall grasses keeps most golfers aiming away from the left side of hole No. 17. (John R. Johnson/golfphotos)

Avoid missing the 17th green to the left. Bunkers and heavy rough lurk there, and on the right is a steep drop-off. (John R. Johnson/golfphotos)

{ THE EIGHTEENTH HOLE }
"Evening Shadows"

PAR 4 | BACK: 382 | MIDDLE: 372 | FORWARD: 352

"It's down the breeze but it doesn't pay at all to go all-out. You might club down but you've got to hit it well down the right side. It requires an honest second shot. I remember that green. Maxwell had a way of building a sort of convex middle of the green, not only for drainage but it also forced you on your second shot to get pin high or just short of pin high."
— BEN CRENSHAW

Another nice wrinkle provided by Perry Maxwell. The fairway is straight but the tee box is offset to the right, so the golfer drives from an angle. That makes it necessary to work the ball from left to right, especially since the heaving fairway surface tilts severely to the left the nearer you get to the green.

Not only is the wind at the golfer's back, but the tee is also elevated, which shortens the hole and makes the bold player go for too much club.

Bunkers and deep rough crowd up against the green on three sides. The front of the green is open, inviting run-up shots. With the approach shot coming from downwind, it requires an understanding of hitting short and allowing the ball to roll toward its final destination.

Like many holes at Prairie Dunes, an understated hole, but certainly a good finishing hole to leave a wonderful memory in the mind of the player.

The 18th hole is played down a valley between the clubhouse on the left and a ridge on the right. The ideal location is the right side of the fairway but everything slants to the left. (Prairie Dunes)

An early view of the clubhouse from the ridge high above the original 9th. (Prairie Dunes)

From the tee, the steep slope to the left is highlighted by evening shadows at hole No. 18. (John R. Johnson/golfphotos)

It is better to risk the trouble in the bunkers up front than to visit the deep rough behind the 18th green. (John R. Johnson/golfphotos)

Chapter Eight

❴ MAJOR EVENTS ❵

Prairie Dunes played a key role in the careers of several of the nation's top golfers. Hall of Fame golfers Jack Nicklaus and Juli Inkster won their first important national events at Prairie Dunes on their way to the top of their professions.

The first tournament with national significance at Prairie Dunes provided lasting memories. It was the 1958 Trans-Mississippi championship won by Nicklaus as he began his climb to the position as a world superstar.

In 1980, Inkster won the U.S. Women's Amateur championship at Prairie Dunes two years before she joined the Ladies Professional Golf Association Tour. It was the first of three consecutive U.S. Amateur titles for Inkster. No other golfer has won three in a row. She was named to the LPGA Hall of Fame in 2000.

Nicklaus was a surprise winner in the 1958 Trans-Miss. Few people had heard of the powerful Ohio teenager at that time. The win paved the way for Nicklaus to be selected to

the 1959 Walker Cup team and earn his first trip overseas for international competition. His Trans-Miss victory came over a field that included Ben Crenshaw, Craig Stadler, Gary Koch, Tom Purtzer, Pete Dye, and two great lifetime amateurs—Richie Norville and Bill Hyndman.

In 1973 Hyndman defeated Norville in the title match when the Trans-Miss returned to Prairie Dunes.

Nicklaus returned in 1962 to play a memorable exhibition match with Arnold Palmer, Prairie Dunes club pro Ross Wilson, and Wichita club pro Gene O'Brien. The exhibition drew a crowd estimated at 4,000.

In that match involving two of the most revered golfers of all time, neither Palmer nor Nicklaus managed to shoot par. Palmer was sailing along until the 340-yard 18th hole, where he drove the ball green high. But he was in the famed Prairie Dunes deep gunsch on the slope of a sand dune right of the green. It took him five more strokes to get down

The crowd watching the 1962 exhibition match featuring Jack Nicklaus and Arnold Palmer. (Prairie Dunes)

Crowd at exhibition match between Arnold Palmer and Jack Nicklaus. From behind the elevated 5th tee looking south toward the fairway. (Prairie Dunes)

from there for a double bogey that resulted in a final score of 72, two over par.

Nicklaus fared even worse. He took a quadruple-bogey 8 on the ninth hole after hacking his way out of the waist-high rough. He finished with a 77.

The women have had a long and distinguished connection with Prairie Dunes. Three U.S. Women's Amateur titles were decided there, and the 1986 Curtis Cup match.

Lifelong amateur Barbara McIntire won her second U.S. Amateur crown at Prairie Dunes in 1964. She was one of only eight women who held the U.S. and British Amateur titles at the same time (1959 and 1960, respectively). In 1956 she tied professional Kathy Cornelius for the lead in the final round of the U.S. Open but lost in a play-off in her bid to become the first amateur to capture the Women's Open crown.

McIntire played on six Curtis Cup teams, captained two others, served on the USGA Women's Committee from 1985 to 1996, and was the chair in 1995 and 1996. The veteran

Judy Bell, Prairie Dunes member and former USGA President. (United States Golf Association)

Curtis Cup player and team captain was named the winner of the 2000 Bob Jones Award, the USGA's highest honor.

In 1991, little Amy Fruhwirth captured the Women's Amateur title with a brilliant display of 4-under-par golf in the final round. The following year she added the 1992 U.S. Public Links championship to her trophy collection before joining the LPGA Tour in 1993.

The U.S. Curtis Cup team that competed at Prairie Dunes in 1986 was captained by Judy Bell, an honorary member of Prairie Dunes who grew up in nearby Wichita and eventually became the first, and to date only, woman president of the USGA in 1996-97.

The 1986 team featured Danielle Ammaccapane, Kim Gardner, Kandi Kessler, Kathleen McCarthy, Dottie Pepper Mochrie, Cindy Schreyer, Leslie Shannon, and Kimberly Williams.

Great Britain and Ireland broke a 13-match losing streak with a 13-5 victory over the U.S. side.

Arnold Palmer slashes his way from the "gunsch" at the 18th hole during his 1962 match with Jack Nicklaus.

Palmer's drive of 340 yards to hole high did not help as he finished with a double bogey six. (Prairie Dunes)

MAJOR EVENTS

Year	Event	Champion
1958	Men's Trans-Mississippi	Jack Nicklaus
1964	U. S. Women's Amateur	Barbara McIntire
1973	Men's Trans-Mississippi	Bill Hyndman
1980	U. S. Women's Amateur	Juli Inkster
1986	24th Curtis Cup Matches	Great Britain-Ireland
1987	Men's Trans-Mississippi	Ron Richard
1988	U.S. Men's Mid-Amateur	David Eger
1991	U.S. Women's Amateur	Amy Fruhwirth
1995	U.S. Men's Senior Amateur	James Stahl Jr.
1996	Men's Trans-Mississippi	John Grace
2002	U.S. Women's Open	